A WORLD TO CONQUER

The Epic Story of the First Around-the-World Flight

ERNEST A. McKAY

ARCO PUBLISHING, INC.
NEW YORK

Published by Arco Publishing, Inc.
219 Park Avenue South, New York, N.Y. 10003

Library of Congress Cataloging in Publication Data

McKay, Ernest A.
   A world to conquer.

   Bibliography: p. 189
    1. Flights around the world. 2. United
States. Army. Air Corps. I. Title.
TL721.U6M34   629.13′09   80-23064
ISBN 0-668-05096-9

Printed in the United States of America

CONTENTS

DEDICATION

For my children, with the hope that they will pursue their
goals with the same determination as the first world fliers.

ACKNOWLEDGMENTS

Special thanks are due Major General Leigh Wade (USAF-Ret.) and Mrs. Lowell Smith who were generous with their time, information and good spirit. Lieutenant General Ira Eaker (USAF-Ret.) and Major General Howard Davidson (USAF-Ret.) were also helpful, and Mrs. Samuel Eaton, daughter of Carlyle Wash, was a kind correspondent. My wife, Ellen, a true partner in this venture, helped with research and sound advice every step of the way.

GEOGRAPHIC NAMES

The geographic names in this book were in common use in 1924. Spelling variations around the world were as frequent then as they are now. For instance, Paramushiru is sometimes seen as Paramushiro. On a grander scale, the identities of many countries have changed. Today, Saigon, now known as Ho Chi Minh City, is in Viet Nam, not French Indo-China. Bangkok is in Thailand, not Siam. Chittagong is in Bangladesh, not Burma. Karachi is in Pakistan, not India. Bushire is in Iran, not Persia; and Baghdad is in Iraq, not Mesopotamia.

I

NO PATH
TO FOLLOW

EVERY DAY of the week, Pan Am Number One takes off from Los Angeles International Airport on its flight around the world. For the passengers, most of whom are well traveled, the event is a routine affair. To the captain and crew it is just one more of many such flights, another day on the job in the latter part of the 20th century when flying long distances *fast* is not news.

As the years fade away and one generation dissolves into another, the origins of settled routine blur. The earlier struggles that carved a pattern are easily forgotten, if they were ever known, and history, an unscientific subject, has a habit of neglecting more than remembering. Lindbergh and Earhart are familiar names, but who first circled the world by air? It's a rare person who knows about an achievement that was as remarkable in its own way as the voyages of Magellan or Drake. Still, dimly or not, we recognize that there must have been someone, somewhere, sometime, who matched his conviction with courage to make us so jaded about today's world flights.

The adventure was a part of the 1920s America that was supposedly turning its back on the world in disillusion. World War I was over and a new age had begun. As everyone knows, tabloids screamed shocking headlines, flappers strutted and jazz came up the river from New Orleans. The young generation was a worry. In the air there were thrills for stunt pilots, wing walkers and the aimless looking for a lark. But this picture is overdrawn. Life was no more a carnival then than it is now. It was not all jazz. Serious men and women set serious goals and among them were skilled aviators who met the increasing demands of their profession. Daring without being foolhardy, they sought engineering and flying techniques that could break through old barriers.

Although no longer an infant, aviation was still a child. The public may have been entranced by its exploits, but for most flying was a pleasure to be enjoyed looking up from the ground. Few had ever flown in a plane and fewer belonged to the select group of record breakers. Everyone was confident of aviation's future, but few faced the problems of the present to reach that bright tomorrow.

In Europe air progress seemed to be advancing more quickly as government support spurred the growth of commercial aviation. Croydon became England's air terminal for traffic with the Continent in 1920; that same year, KLM began regular flights between Rotterdam and London. More than 15,000 paying passengers had crossed the English Channel by 1924 and airlines had direct connections with most continental capitals. Berlin was only 24 hours from Moscow. The political implications were clear as one nation vied with another for supremacy in the air. Benito Mussolini, a new premier growing in confidence, sought a place in the sky to bolster Italy's prestige as a Mediterranean power. He wanted enough planes to hide the sun by 1925. France spent three million dollars a year in subsidies, and Great Britain gave financial aid to the new Imperial Airways.

Commercial aviation lagged behind in the United States. There were no air regulations and no subsidies. The American spirit of free enterprise in those neo-laissez-faire days opposed government interference and there were no friendly gestures in the direction of passenger-carrying airlines. Motor boats were inspected and certified, but decrepit airplanes and incompetent pilots remained unchallenged.

Still, all was not hopeless. The United States Air Mail Service was flying nearly two million miles a year with unparalleled safety and regularity while their pilots learned hard lessons for the future. And the small air services in the dwindling peacetime Army and Navy did impressive work in research and design. Their unheralded efforts in metallurgy, meteorology and physics influenced the construction and operation of early aircraft.

The new Army Air Service, made up of men from all walks of life, some with commissions and some without, monopolized most of the world records for altitude, speed, endurance and distance. Major General Mason Patrick, Chief of the Air Service, thought a good method to battle low budgets was to enter aeronautical events to attract national attention. By 1923, only 14 years after the Signal Corps bought its first workable plane, the Army had chalked up some remarkable records. In 1919, Lt. Colonel R. S. Hartz and Lieutenant E. E. Harmon made a complete circuit of the United States, a distance of 9823 miles, in a Martin bomber. In 1920, four wood and wire Army planes flew from New York to Nome, Alaska, and back without a mishap. In 1922, Lieutenant James Doolittle, a promising young flier, made the first coast to coast flight in a single day. In 1923, Lieutenants John Macready and

Oakley Kelly flew a single engine Fokker T-2 non-stop from New York to San Diego to set "The Greatest Record of All."

But the Air Service was a dangerous place to work. Combat, pursuit and scouting included tail spins, nose dives, loops and Immelmann turns as normal tactical training. Ninety-two percent of the sudden and violent deaths in the peacetime Army of 1921 occurred in the small Air Service. In one year there were 330 crashes in an air force of fewer than 900 pilots and observers. Someone calculated that in proportion to size, the percentage of deaths in the aviation branch was 4200 percent over the average for all other branches and a commissioned air officer would be killed 2.4 times and maimed .8 times before he reached retirement in 30 years. And the single promotion list, that benefited other branches as air casualties created vacancies, did not help morale. Requests for transfer into the Air Service dropped as the World War I attitude of "we who are about to die salute you" faded. The Lassiter Committee, a board of General Staff officers, reported to the War Department that an "alarming condition in the air service exists, due to shortage of flying personnel and equipment."

With all of the risks, there were those who loved to fly and, more important, understood flying. They put dismal statistics out of their minds and went to work. These were the men who wanted to be the first to fly around the world. Even in 1923 the idea was not new, but the accumulation of long distance overseas flights made the dream seem increasingly possible. A Navy plane, NC-4, with Lt. Commander Albert C. Read and his crew had managed to cross the Atlantic via the Azores, and the able Australian brothers, Ross and Keith Smith, had flown from London to Melbourne. The Smiths, always adventurous, had thought about circumnavigating the globe in 1921, but Ross had a fatal crash in a Vimy at Brooklands, England. Other attempts had been made, only to end in failure. Nevertheless, there was no shortage of contestants. The British, French, Portuguese, Italians and Argentinians were among those who publicly declared their intentions. Commandante Sacadura Cabral, an experienced Portuguese aviator, bought a Fokker biplane with a Rolls-Royce engine and dreamed of following Magellan's route.

As early as 1922, Major Herbert Dargue, the Chief of War Plans Section of the Air Service, discussed a world flight which was shelved that summer because of the negative attitude of the General Staff. The hostility of the General Staff was mostly a matter of money. In the Harding and Coolidge era there was always a scramble for a share of the small appropriations, and the cavalry, artillery and other traditional branches seemed to have the better of the bargain. When Coolidge moved into the White House a popular story circulated around Washington that the President had asked the Secretary of War, "What's all this talk about lots of airplanes? Why not buy one airplane and let the Army pilots take turns flying it."

Frustrated in their demands and dissatisfied with the lack of sympathy from the General Staff for their projects, the men of the Air Service sometimes came close to developing a sense of persecution. If nothing else, it sharpened the camaraderie in an outfit where almost everyone knew everyone else. Quick to defend their views, they used their own resources to advance their missions. The air officers knew that their jobs had glamour and they looked for support from the public. More than one newspaperman found himself taken on a free plane ride. These fliers were playing a young man's game, their adventures appealed to the public and they knew that the future belonged to them.

Advocates of the world flight included Brigadier General Billy Mitchell, the Assistant Chief of Air Service, a man who had a talent for causing commotion and generating publicity. Mitchell, the son of a United States Senator and grandson of a western tycoon, spoke loud and often about the importance of air power, frequently to the discomfort of his superiors. In principle he was often right; in practice he might have been more effective if he had ruffled fewer feathers. The sinking of overage battleships in bombing tests off the Virginia Capes was one of his recent undertakings. It gave him opportunities to snipe at the Navy, feed the press headlines and create enemies as well as an abundance of admirers. The young officers in the Air Service who never had to cross his path idolized him. To them, the personable general did everything just right. Aside from being an expert flier, he spoke well, wrote well and was a great outdoorsman.

Mitchell believed in taking the case for military aviation directly to Congress and the people and ignoring the General Staff. In October 1922, Mitchell told a newspaperman, "I am arranging for a 'round-the-world flight with a squadron of six planes." When the remark appeared in the press, the Deputy Chief of Staff called Major General Patrick on the carpet and demanded to know what was going on. Both men knew that the flight had not been approved. Placed in an awkward position, Patrick issued a statement to calm the waters and at the same time show that he was Mitchell's commander. "By *my* direction," he said, "one of

the divisions in *my* office has been giving study to possible long flights."
For the time being, the matter rested there.

Mitchell might steal headlines, but he could not claim credit for spearheading the world flight. In the fall of 1923, he received generous orders for an inspection tour that took him to the Far East. The orders, designed to get him out of the country and out of the newspapers for awhile, fit into his personal plans since he was about to marry for a second time. In Siam, Mitchell would not be able to resist intimating that he was there in connection with a proposed world flight. However, the Chargé d'Affaires soon realized, much to his annoyance, that the newlyweds were more interested in tiger hunts.

It was the more moderate Patrick, often overshadowed by the "martyr for air power," who bore the brunt for a 1923 proposal that ran up against many cross currents. The son of a surgeon in the Confederate Army, he had a keen mind and was not unaccustomed to weaving his way through an organization rife with jealousies. General Pershing had appointed him Chief of Air Service of the American Expeditionary Force in 1918 when he tired of wartime squabbles between airmen who did not like taking orders from ground officers who had never flown a plane, and ground officers who looked upon airmen as too temperamental. Even worse, some of the leading airmen had trouble working among themselves. Mitchell, with all of the irritating qualities of a man who was always sure that he was right, fought bitterly with his superior, Brigadier General Benjamin Foulois, the first Army flier, who thought Mitchell's staff work was totally inept.

Patrick, an engineering officer with a reputation as a stern disciplinarian, was more than reluctant to accept the assignment. When he said that he had paid little attention to aviation, Pershing replied, "Never mind, I think you can do the job. It needs a strong hand and a man who can see far." He was right. Patrick's talent for organization brought some order to the strife in France. After the war he was brought back again when Major General Menoher resigned in another feud with Mitchell. Patrick's job was to restore discipline to the Air Service. One of his biggest problems was to keep Mitchell in line while giving him enough rope to help promote air power. Young Captain Ira Eaker, later organizer of the VIII Bomber Command during World War II, occupied an office between the two generals—the only generals in the Air Service—and often heard their clashes. While Mitchell spoke out for a separate air force, Patrick proceeded in a more practical fashion through the organization. He hoped that someday he might build a corps within the Army comparable to the Marines in the Navy Department. Realizing the irony of a ground officer heading the Air Service, he insisted upon qualifying as a pilot at the age of 60.

Patrick did not think that Congress would support the Air Service unless he could show that aviation had capabilities far beyond the battle-line of armies and navies. That was a good reason for proposing the world flight. On the other hand, there were plenty of reasons for oppos-ing a world flight. The obstacles seemed insurmountable. The weather, equipment limitations, inexperienced pilots, poor communications and lack of bases were among countless considerations. Each was a threat to success, and failure would be a disaster for an already weak Air Service. Yet each obstacle was a reason for the attempt. It was both difficult and enticing for the simple reason that it had never been done. That was what it was all about. To try to overcome the obstacles was the purpose of the flight. But there were other more subtle blocks. Within the Army itself there were conflicting interests that touched the project. Under-lying the apparently innocent plan lurked the possibility that a success-ful journey would help promote the idea of an independent air force. That thought did not appeal to the Army General Staff. Then there was a competitive service plan. The Navy had its own ideas about a flight around the world.

Rear Admiral W. A. Moffett, Chief of the Bureau of Aeronautics, a man who hid his ability under a mild manner, outlined the objectives of a global flight via Honolulu, Midway, Wake and Guam with 21 station ships to take off about February 1, 1924. He was already thinking about the next war and presented a sound rationale. Naval strategists claimed that aircraft were vital to future war plans even though no one really knew whether or not they were capable of operating with the fleet anywhere in the world. In a letter to the Secretary of the Navy he wrote, "We *think* we shall be able to operate aircraft with the fleet anywhere in the world by the time the next war comes along, but we haven't *proved* it. It's high time we started to prove it, before we go too far in placing reliance on aircraft. Maybe we are placing too much faith in air-craft, maybe we aren't placing enough." He thought that the quickest way to find out whether or not planes could go anywhere in the world was to send them there. The flight would tell them in no uncertain terms what they wanted to know. He wanted to determine the ability of aircraft to find their way across open sea, to find out the efficiency of the power plants and to test the durability of the men and materials. He wanted to judge results, not potential. Tests at home only demonstrated potential.

The astute Moffett was as aware of the political side as Patrick. He knew that there was interest in organizing an air service in the United States similar to the new Royal Air Force which had kicked up so much bitterness in England. The Joint Board had opposed such a move, but under the surface there was strong sentiment in the country for a combined and independent air force. In the battle for a separate service the Admirals were cast in the public mind as old fogeys opposed to the development of aviation. "It matters not," wrote Moffett, "that this impression is way wide of the actual truth of the matter. The impression exists very widely, and the Navy suffers because of it. It so happens that the Air Service of the Army, or at least the influential officers in it, are strong advocates of the separate air service idea and no opportunity is overlooked in the Air Service publicity campaign to belittle the efforts or effectiveness of the Navy, or to place the separate air force idea in the most favorable light before the public."

Moffett was dedicated to aviation and had often defended Mitchell as a fellow proponent of air power, but by now he had grown weary of the general's headline hunting, arrogance and self-righteousness. Mitchell had embarrassed the Navy too many times without understanding their problems. He was also too anxious to set up a separate air force to suit loyal Navy men.

Moffett knew about the Army plans for a world flight and they annoyed him. He knew that they did not have the equipment to follow the route proposed by the Navy and, besides, the oceans were Navy territory. Even more irritating, the planes the Army planned to use were, with a few modifications, a direct copy of torpedo planes the Navy had developed. Exasperated, he asked, "Can we afford to let the Army beat us to a 'round the world flight, and place in the hands of the separate Air Force proponents an argument that the Navy left it to the land lubber to show the possibilities in one of the strongest potential weapons in warfare?" Emotions ran high. The admiral's frank discussion gave added significance and impetus to the world flight plans.

International and interservice rivalries were strong undercurrents that swept competitors toward the flight. There was no doubt that Americans wanted to be first or that the Army would take delight in beating the Navy in the air race to conquer the world. To a degree that was good.

From the time of the Wright brothers, air progress had been based on competition with races, meets, challenges, trophies and cash spurring innovation. As long as the competition did not become too bitter, it served a useful purpose.

Moffett was right. Many influential officers in the Army Air Service harbored the idea of an independent force. They saw opportunities for developing new strategies and tactics on their own. And they saw the possibilities for more rapid promotion. But most officers were not in a position to make a public stand on such a controversial topic. Only a Mitchell, with independent means and political connections, could afford the luxury of arousing the ire of his superiors. Any mention of an ulterior motive would have to be left out of a serious rationale for an Army world flight.

Favorable publicity for the Army Air Service was another, more modest aim for a world flight. Imaginative flying officers could easily envision the newspaper space that would be devoted to what seemed like the ultimate achievement. The Air Service had seen what lesser achievements had done to build public interest in aviation in general and Army aviation in particular. But creating a good press was self-serving and suspect for any official proposal. Headlines might lead to bigger budgets, but it was an argument better left unsaid. It was one more unmentionable.

Politics and publicity were put aside as the air staff prepared its case. Surprisingly, the Army Air Service, unlike the Navy, did not talk about war aims. It could have argued that the flight could help develop techniques for the next war. Long distance flying to test the feasibility of long range bombing runs might have been offered as a reason, or testing the endurance of pilots for future combat. They were not. Instead, the objectives of the mission were spelled out in peaceful terms. This may have simply been good thinking in a nation tired of war, but it also made good sense. Their first interest was to find out more about the business of flying. Indirectly, of course, this would eventually affect military aviation.

The flight's immediate concerns were distance, time, climate and airways. Working under Lt. Colonel J. E. Fechet, later Chief of the Army Air Service, the staff proposed a world flight simply to gain experience in long-distance flying. That meant much more than hours in the air. Flying long distances required ground support and supply. Little was known about landing areas and logistics, especially in far away places.

In 1924, there were few airfields in the United States, much less in far from home and often uncivilized locations.

The mission's second objective was to complete the flight in "the shortest practicable time." Speed in itself was not the issue. It was a matter of time in relation to safety. The Air Service had no intention of flashing from one country to another around the globe. In a preliminary way, they were thinking of completing the flight in months, not days.

Another reason for the flight was to demonstrate the feasibility of establishing an airway around the world. At the time there was no path to follow. In Europe and the United States there were a few limited airways that might be useful. All else was largely unknown. An air route with emergency landing fields, beacon lights and radio beams was far in the future. Exploring the possibility of a world airway was probably the most farsighted of their objectives. The Air Service knew that any first flight would only touch upon the complex problems of building international airways. But it would be a beginning. Army aviators were aware that such airways were vital to the growth of commercial aviation and the military services needed the support of private industry if they expected to grow. Airways would lead to the development of airlines that would build public confidence and grant contracts to commercial aircraft builders. The Army Air Service did not construct their own planes and their funds for research and development were never sufficient. Private industry had to advance new ideas, new designs and new models. If a flight could show that an airway around the world was possible, even at some remote date, commercial aviation would receive a big boost. The aviation industry would raise their sights and that would mean more help for the Army Air Service.

There was also a need to know more about operating aircraft in various climates. Technically, this was probably the most important reason for the flight. No one knew if an airplane had been built that could withstand the extremes of both heat and cold. Many experts were skeptical. They did not believe that the frame or fabric could take the sharp changes in environment. What would happen to the wings or fuselage if the temperature dropped from 100 degrees or more to zero or less? What effect would it have on the engine? There were other questions related to winds, heavy air, light air and humidity. Certainly, whatever the route, a world flight would test the limits of an aircraft under varying conditions.

Finally, since a world flight was a common conversation piece among adventurous aviators of all nations, almost all of them realized that it would probably become an accomplished fact in the very near future. No one could deny the dramatic appeal of the great challenge to be first. Still, the Army didn't try to capitalize on this appeal to nationalism. Only as a last point in their objectives was it stated that they "incidentally" wished to gain the honor for the United States of being the first nation to circle the world by air.

General Patrick presented the objectives his staff had spelled out to Secretary of War Weeks and an indifferent Congress, and his diplomacy won the day. Though the flight would take money, and the cost-conscious President, ever vigilant about unnecessary government expenditures, could have blocked the plan, he did not. Perhaps his Yankee curiosity got the better of him.

Moffett's proposal for a Navy flight, on the other hand, went into the Secretary of the Navy's file, never to appear again. Perhaps the Secretary was too preoccupied with the bad publicity of the Teapot Dome scandal to concentrate on a world flight scheme. The Senate would soon be calling for his resignation for signing oil leases and contracts. More likely, the Navy airmen suffered from a lack of single purpose. Another plan, to send the airship *Shenandoah* to the North Pole, seemed more important to many of them. Time and again, airships were compared with ocean liners and some Navy men were sure that within a few years long-distance travel by dirigible would be a certainty. One of the navigating officers of the *Shenandoah* proudly claimed that a cruise in the skies on an airship produced none of that bumpy airplane motion and soon there would be lighter-than-air aircraft routes all over the world. Moffett's own faith in dirigibles would be fatal. In 1933 he would go down with the airship *Akron* when it crashed off the New Jersey coast.

The Army Air Service had the approval they had so earnestly desired. The purpose was clear, but how could it be accomplished?

II

THE PLANNERS

THERE WAS nothing devil-may-care in the Air Service's attitude as they set to work. The first step was to form a World Flight Committee in the Training and War Plans Division in Washington. The chairman, First Lieutenant Robert J. Brown, Jr., gathered around him five other experienced officers, each with specific responsibilities, who tackled a myriad of details to develop a plan. A primitive forerunner of space-age programming was in the making as the committee faced the problems of maps, routes, equipment, engineering and supply.

No anticipated detail was overlooked. The problem was what to anticipate. There were so many questions and so few answers. What kind of airplane could withstand the extremes in temperature? Were landing facilities available at reasonable distances? Where would they find fuel? Was air navigation possible over long distances over water? Could pilots endure the pressures? Worst of all, what would the pilots do if they arrived at one of the unfamiliar destinations and it was covered by fog? Could they land? No one knew.

The flight circled a different world than we know today. The Japanese, rather than the Russians, controlled the Kurile Islands in the northern Pacific, Americans thrived in a chaotic China and the French dominated Indo-China and Syria. The British Empire may have reached its peak in the latter part of the 19th century, but their paramount interests, mandates and protectorates all gave a semblance of power in the huge expanse of southern Asia and the Middle East.

The committee divided this world into six divisions with an advance officer assigned to each division. In the summer of 1923, Weeks asked Secretary of State Charles Evans Hughes for help in obtaining clearances in 22 foreign countries for both the pathfinders and the world fliers. Paving the way diplomatically for credentials and free passage of the flight was a mammoth assignment. Embassies and legations around the world spent months in paperwork and negotiations to lay the groundwork and clear up misunderstandings.

Most nations expressed a willingness to cooperate, but they had suspicions and questions as well as exceptions and conditions. Flying over army and navy installations and aerial photography were favorite topics for discussion. Then there was bureaucratic lethargy where no real problem existed. For months there were various stages of confirmation or misgivings that defied a final settlement. The vast correspondence file in the State Department in Washington grew larger and larger.

Canada gave immediate approval and the Governor General instructed officers of the Royal Canadian Air Force to render every possible assistance. Denmark offered a cruising warship in the North Atlantic to serve as a radio station. There were other equally helpful nations. Among the more troublesome was the "friendly" Chinese government at Peking which rejected passage because its miniscule Aviation Department objected to the military character of the aircraft. Eventually, when it was explained that the planes would carry no weapons, the Chinese reluctantly agreed to ten stipulations that forbade photographic and wireless equipment, low flying and scattering anything from the air. The American foreign service officers did not think that the conditions were too onerous and even questioned whether they would be enforced. Actually, the restrictions were later modified, but the negotiations took time.

Turkey stubbornly refused permission for the flight and asked to be omitted from the itinerary because they could not assure the safety of the machines. The excuse was transparent, but the objection persisted. As late as February 1924 there was a real possibility that an alternative flight plan to Paris via Egypt, Greece and Italy would have to be adopted. It would be 1500 miles longer and far more dangerous. At the last moment Turkey gave in with the understanding that their military officers could inspect the planes on arrival.

In some instances governments objected to proposed routes. India suggested an alternate route that forced extra studies and detailed agreements. Rumania never gave more than verbal permission. So it went.

Whatever troubles foreign service officers encountered, they were nothing compared with the difficulties in Japan. When William Phillips, writing for the Secretary of State in late August, instructed the embassy in Tokyo to request permission for pathfinders, John MacMurray, the Far East Expert, noted, "This matter of foreign aircraft in Japan is a matter of such degree of suspicion and chauvinistic nationalism as can be scarcely understood by those who have not had experience of the abnormal psychology of the Japanese in regard to questions of 'national defense.' " In November the embassy at Tokyo was still waiting for a reply from the Foreign Office.

Near the end of November, Jefferson Caffery, the suave Chargé d'Affaires ad interim in Tokyo, informally asked the Vice Minister for Foreign Affairs for his personal opinion about the probable attitude of the Japanese authorities. A few days later the minister told Caffery that, quite frankly, the War Office did not look favorably on the flight. Nevertheless, he had a suggestion. He advised the American Government not to urge the Japanese Government too strongly. Then, under such circumstances, he did not believe that the War Office would raise objections. This reverse strategy had its limitations. Time was running out. Caffery went away hoping for a more definite answer the next day. It was not forthcoming.

The American Military Attaché at Tokyo tried his hand at another approach. He called on the private secretary of the Minister of War, a close friend of several years, and asked him what was holding up the project. He was told that the Japanese General Staff opposed the flight for many reasons. The United States, he bluntly said, was not a signatory to the International Air Agreement, the planes were military and, most important, a flight from the Aleutians to the Kuriles to Hokkaido would be a probable route for an air invasion from America. It was clear that the Japanese did not want Americans scouting their northern islands.

The American Attaché replied that it would be unfortunate if Japan were the cause for abandoning the flight. It would only furnish more fuel for American newspaper fires. Although he did not say so, it was well known that the Hearst papers, based in California, were emphasizing the "yellow peril" and Billy Mitchell was making headlines with claims that war with Japan was inevitable. All that the Army fliers sought, though, was the most practical way across the Pacific.

Looking back, it seemed to the people at the American Embassy that the proposal had not taken into account Japanese attitudes. They now felt that it would have been better to request general permission to fly over Japan before taking up the subject of the pathfinders. But it was too late now as they waited for an answer.

On the morning of December 8, 1923, the Military Attaché called by appointment at the War Office and was told that there was no objection to the flight on the condition that the first stop would be Honshu Island. It was, of course, an absurd answer since this route bypassed all the northern islands and forced the fliers to make a non-stop, 1200 mile jump. In the afternoon, Caffery learned that the Foreign Office had asked the War Office to reconsider this impossible restriction and suggested two intermediate stops. The War Office promised to reconsider, but Caffery was not optimistic about the outcome. In the evening, the private secretary of the Minister of War visited the embassy to say that if the Americans considered the flight from the Aleutians to Honshu too long, Japan would be disposed to accept an intermediate stop at Shimushu Island in the Kuriles. This was progress of sorts, but the distance was still too great. The Japanese seemed to take pleasure in toying with the Americans while trying to learn the distance capability of the planes.

On January 9, 1923, Caffery advised the Secretary of State that Japanese approval had been received with the understanding that the only landing place permitted on the flight from the Aleutians to Honshu would be Shimushu and that details relating to fortified zones and naval stations would be settled between the Japanese military authorities and an American officer detailed for that purpose. The Japanese also expected a reciprocal agreement for any flight that they might make over American territory. This was not a perfect agreement, but it opened the way for more detailed talks. On January 17, the Japanese further agreed to a landing at Bettobu in the Kuriles. Although the trouble was not over, at least the door was ajar enough for the advance officer to commence work.

THE ADVANCE OFFICERS had a key role in planning and supporting the flight. This wasn't an easy job. The pathfinders were all experienced aviators selected because they knew how to get things done. They sought landing areas four to five hundred miles apart, mapped routes over seas, valleys and mountain ranges and checked a long list of particulars that included the magnetic declination, velocity of wind at which landing was possible and depth of water at mean low tide. They also set up lines of radio communication, shipped supplies to isolated places, selected local agents and organized bases. After shepherding the flight through their division, they would be responsible for paying the bills and returning surplus supplies. These details would make the difference between success and failure, and it is impossible to magnify the importance of these men and the job they did.

The treacherous First Division, assigned to First Lieutenant Clayton L. Bissell, extended from Seattle, Washington, to Attu at the far western tip of the Aleutians. One of the hottest pilots in the 148th Aero Squadron, Bissell had downed five enemy planes during the war. Soon after the first of the year, hardly the most propitious season for trudging through Alaska, he started his survey. Nothing seemed to discourage the hard-working Bissell as he talked to people familiar with local weather conditions, checked the number of months the ground was frozen, the date of thaw, the opening of water transportation, searched for aircraft facilities and emergency machine shops, set storage places for provisions and tried to train uninterested natives in some simple duties.

First Lieutenant Clifford C. Nutt, a veteran of the New York to Nome flight, now stationed in the Philippines, was advance officer for the Second Division that stretched throughout Japan. As soon as Caffery completed diplomatic arrangements, Nutt proceeded to Tokyo. The lieutenant arrived on February 6 and found himself up against a committee of 14 Army and Navy officers headed by Major General Yasumitsu, commander of the Japanese Air Service. It was an imposing group.

At the first meeting, Nutt asked for permission for the flight to land at selected points in the Kuriles. He received a point-blank refusal—not a good beginning. As a counter proposal, the Japanese said that since the American planes could fly 2200 miles there was no necessity for landing in Japan. It was obvious that they had kept up with American news releases. The aircraft's 2200 mile range had been mentioned in papers across the country. This figure was a theoretical maximum, and Nutt tried to explain that this cruising radius was an exaggeration and that his orders were to plan flights of no more than 500 miles. General Yasumitsu signaled the end of the meeting and told Nutt that the committee would send for him when they reached a decision. Almost a week passed before he heard from them again.

At the next meeting Nutt presented an alternate flight plan that would not land or pass within five miles of any fortified area. The committee was still not pleased. In their most patronizing manner they said that Americans had such wonderfully designed planes and experienced pilots that a forced landing was impossible and it would be a waste of time to make flights of less than 1000 miles. Nutt answered that if the pilots could not land every 500 miles to check their planes and rest, the flight could not pass through Japan successfully. After much argument, he was told that the committee would discuss the route and inform him later.

To help the American case, the State Department forwarded a long list of courtesies in military affairs that had been extended to the Japanese. It included the attendance of their Assistant Naval Attachés at the bombing of the *Ostfriesland* in a test off the Virginia Capes, and later the bombings of the overage ships *Virginia* and *New Jersey*.

Several days later, the committee accepted a route with two stops in the Kuriles and another at Minato on the way to Tokyo. An alteration had been made to avoid the Ominato naval base which the Americans might, "unintentionally of course," fly over. South of Tokyo, Kushimoto replaced Osaka as a landing area. The Japanese had no objection to landing at Osaka, but it would be necessary to fly there by a circuitous route to keep clear of several military areas. Other restrictions prohibited photographic equipment, flying within five miles of land except when approaching or leaving a harbor and flying within 15 miles of any fortified area. Nutt agreed to the changes and then attempted to talk about arrangements for each stop. He was told that would be taken up at the next meeting. After a lengthy discussion among themselves, it was announced that a Japanese pilot would have to fly in the leader's plane to guide the flight. Nutt patiently explained that there was no room for a third person. He suggested that they guide the flight with one of their own planes. No more was heard of the subject.

The next four or five meetings discussed ways to establish bases in the Kuriles. Nutt tried to charter a boat for supplies but had no success in finding anyone who would make the dangerous trip before April 15. One Japanese firm replied, "This journey must be undertaken by those who are prepared to die." It was hardly encouraging. Nutt intimated to the committee that the only solution was to send American destroyers. They countered with an offer to send two of their own destroyers which would carry 1000 gallons of gasoline, about half the supply required. Nutt did not push his request too hard at the time for fear of a definite refusal.

Major General Patrick received conference reports in Washington and grew anxious. He advised Nutt through the State Department that it was essential to complete arrangements for the Kuriles by April 15 at the latest. When he received the message, Nutt requested that the committee convene again to reach a decision. By this time the British asked to be present because they were having troubles with their own proposed world flight. Nutt was sure that the committee sensed a showdown. In addition to the regular committee there were 14 or 15 representatives of the Foreign Office present.

Nutt didn't waste any time. He gave the committee the cable he had received and explained that none of the plans outlined so far met the requirements of the flight, that time was short and they must decide upon a definite plan now. He offered two possible plans. The first was that the Japanese carry all of the supplies on two destroyers with an American officer on each to be on station by April 15. The Japanese said that was impossible since no ship could reach the northern Kuriles before April 26 because of ice-clogged waters. Nutt's second plan was for two American destroyers to visit the Kuriles and care for the flight. This would relieve the Japanese, he said, of all responsibility for the safety of the flight and save them the expense of sending their ships. The British chimed in and said that if the Americans were allowed in the Kuriles their ships should receive the same privileges.

Arguments flew back and forth as the Japanese put forth several impossible plans that Nutt turned down as impractical. Members of the Foreign Office finally agreed to persuade the War Office to accept one of Nutt's two plans. The tense meeting started at 11:00 A.M. and lasted five hours. As the members left, Nutt asked Commander Hara, the ranking officer on the naval side of the committee, to try to give him an answer the next day. The same evening, Hara and Colonel Obata, another member of the committee, called on Nutt in his room at the Imperial Hotel. They told him that after much heated discussion the War Office had decided to wash their hands of the whole affair and allow the American destroyers to take care of the matter, provided that one Japanese Army and one Navy pilot traveled with them and they touched only the designated points in the Kuriles at Bettobu and Kashiwabara. Obata said that both the committee and the War Office were "fed up" with the whole proposition and that it would be useless to ask for anything more. Nutt soon realized that Obata surprisingly did not present an exact picture of their attitude. When the Japanese reconciled themselves to the American determination, they did an about-face and from then on did everything in their power to help. Nevertheless, it had been a nerve-wracking few months.

Two other officers in the Philippines were to cover the Third and Fourth Divisions. They had problems too. When the planes left Japan,

First Lieutenant Malcolm Lawton would be responsible for the route through China and southeast Asia to Calcutta, India. First Lieutenant Harold Halverson would pick up the section from Calcutta to Constantinople, Turkey. While Bissell suffered with the cold, Lawton and Halverson suffered with the heat. The route across Europe to London, the Fifth Division, was in the hands of Major Carlyle Wash, Assistant Military Attaché for Aviation in Paris. Crossing the Atlantic was the concern of First Lieutenant Clarence Crumrine, another veteran of the New York to Nome flight.

Each advance officer's problems were distinct. Lawton left for Peking about the middle of March and upon arrival found that China was primitive flying country. Air travel, commercial or military, was almost nonexistent and there were few people to supply competent information. Air notes, maps and sketches of landing areas were almost nonexistent. Questionnaires previously sent out from Washington seeking detailed answers about flying conditions were incompletely filled out by consuls who freely admitted that they lacked the technical knowledge needed to make them worthwhile. There was a landing field at Shanghai, but no regular service. The same was true at Canton. In Burma, which was also Lawton's territory, there were no suitable fields at all. The flight could save time if it changed from pontoons to wheels, but leveling croplands to make landing strips was prohibitively expensive. It soon became obvious that landings would have to be made on water along the coast. Traveling great distances, often under hazardous circumstances, Lawton found that his best assistance came from the United States Navy, Standard Oil agents who were old China hands and, in Indo-China, the French Air Service.

Harry Halverson, later one of the pilots of the *Question Mark* that set a well-publicized endurance record in 1929, searched for landing areas from Calcutta through the Middle East. His instructions were to find runways one and a half the length necessary for a normal takeoff because of the planes' anticipated weight. He found it tough enough to find runways of any size, much less extra long ones that didn't have plane-crippling craters in the middle. The RAF was extremely cooperative, but they did not operate everywhere along the line of flight.

To make matters worse, communications were terrible. In Persia, the wireless did not work at Chahbar or Bandar Abbas, and behaved erratically at Bushire. Sleeping accommodations were almost nil, disease was rampant and at Chahbar there was little food.

Major Wash, an ex-cavalry officer who vowed he would never ride another horse after duty on the Mexican border, quickly admitted that he had an easier assignment than the other advance officers. It seemed to be part of his nature to give credit to others, but he did not do himself justice. He did not have to struggle with ice and snow, heat exhaustion or disease. More important, he did not have to chart new air routes or improvise landing facilities. Except for Turkey, the governments he dealt with were friendly. Nevertheless, Wash worked in eight countries with seven different languages, and sometimes civilization created its own problems.

Most of the time, Wash worked outside of the various governments because the Compagnie Franco Roumaine de Navigation Aerienne offered their services on the Continent and Air Union promised to aid the flight to England. These pioneering commercial airlines had already established airways. Franco Roumaine had founded a line from Paris to Strasbourg in 1920 and gradually extended its operations to Istanbul via Innsbruck, Vienna, Budapest, Belgrade and Bucharest.

Perhaps Wash's most courageous act was to fly the Franco Roumaine route. The airline's careless maintenance, over-used engines and lethargic personnel did not exactly give passengers a sense of security. He flew in two tri-motored planes that seemed to eat up oil and were covered with oil and dirt. He noticed that they used castor oil, which was more expensive and less efficient than mineral oil, and he had trouble accepting the rickety airline as a serious commercial venture. The aircraft were too heavy and too high in horsepower, he thought, for the small amount of passenger traffic. The company had acquired six Caudron C 61s in 1923. They had three Hispano-Suiza eight-cylinder engines, each producing 180 horsepower. Within the fuselage there was room for eight passengers, with the crew of two flying the plane from an open cockpit. Wash thought they would have been wiser to concentrate on mail and express service. It took mail seven or eight days to reach Paris from Constantinople, even though a train could make the distance in about three and a half days, and telegraphic service was even worse—a telegram might reach Paris in three or four days or perhaps never at all. Even if Franco Roumaine was missing a sterling opportunity, Wash was indebted to them for their friendly cooperation.

The advance work gave the sharp-eyed Wash an opportunity to view post-war Europe. As a military attaché he did not forget that he was an intelligence officer and he carefully observed conditions in each of the countries he visited. That was his job and he was not optimistic about what he saw. In his opinion, Vienna was dark, dull and disappointing. Even if it was the seat of the new Federal Government of Austria, it no longer seemed the sparkling capital of mid-Europe. Bucharest, the "Paris of the Balkans," was a straggling village in the midst of a great dusty plain that did not live up to its reputation. Corruption in government was everywhere. From the Bosphorus, Constantinople looked like the most beautiful city in the world. Within the gates the illusion faded. Wash regarded the Turks as dangerous people because their fanaticism was intense and their ignorance vast. The danger was diluted by the corruption of the ruling class, inertia and inefficiency. The only city that appealed to him was Budapest. He found the Hungarian vitality made the city lively even though it was sternly ruled by a dictator, Admiral Horthy.

Wash concluded that all in all, the war for peace had failed in that part of the world. The Treaty of Versailles satisfied no one and the principle of self-determination caused great mischief. The Turkish belief in their invincibility, the growing Bolshevism in Bulgaria and Rumania, the spirit of revenge that Bulgaria held against Rumania, the animosity between Italy and Yugoslavia and the belligerence between Czechoslovakia and Poland (fostered by French influence and money) appeared to him to be building toward another Balkan War.

Lieutenant Crumrine, unlike Wash, had little opportunity to observe politics. He spent the summer and winter of 1923 exploring Greenland, Iceland and the Faeroe Islands. No airplane had ever flown across the Atlantic from east to west, but he was convinced that there were several possible landing areas on the west coast of Greenland and that even the east coast of that barren land might offer a haven. His optimism was not shared by some Danish skeptics who believed that it would be too cold even in summer.

Meanwhile, in Washington, D.C., First Lieutenant St. Clair Streett pored over maps and charts and made the world flight on paper. No ordinary desk officer, Streett had led the flight from New York to Nome in 1920 without a mishap. He understood the importance of this endless collecting of details. He also had a streak of daring. Once when flying almost wing-to-wing with Mitchell, Mitchell had circled the Washington Monument as a challenge to the younger officer. Streett accepted the challenge and did him one better by making a steep bank and flying around the shaft within a few feet of it.

Streett was the committee member responsible for the route. He collected information from every available source. Military attachés at embassies throughout the world filed preliminary reports on possible routes that supplemented the work of the advance officers. Even Foulois, now on duty in Berlin, was pleased to contribute to the mission by collecting information from his Luftwaffe friends. The Navy Department Hydrographic Office furnished 1:16 scale charts for coasts where there might be pontoon landings. The Coast and Geodetic Survey supplied maps of British Columbia, the Alaskan coasts and the Aleutian Islands. British, German and Danish Admiralty charts and maps were studied for the Faeroes, Greenland and Labrador. There were also conferences with Coast Guard officers, traders and explorers to learn more about specific situations. More information came from the Bureau of Fisheries and the National Geographic Society. Even the Associated Chamber of Commerce of China offered help. The Pacific and Atlantic Ocean Pilot Books of the United States Navy and Great Britain were a big help, too. Streett, Brown and the other planners, all meticulous men, tried not to overlook anything. Eventually, after hours of study, Streett prepared an airway guidebook and maps for the world fliers.

Many theories existed about the best route around the world. The one finally selected for the American attempt surprised even experienced aviators when they learned that it proceeded west instead of east. This seemed like swimming upstream since the prevailing winds throughout the entire world were generally from the west and it was known that the well-publicized English and Portuguese world flights would go with the westerlies. The contrary American decision was not taken lightly. The planning committee's idea was that the worst of the winter would be over when the fliers flew up the brutal Alaskan coast in April and May, that they would beat the June typhoons in the Yellow Sea and China, miss most of the rain in India and escape the harshest of the seasons in the North Atlantic. It was a sound theory, but would it work in practice? The Europeans had a great advantage. Their starting point in April would give them the same edge in weather flying with the westerlies that the Americans were trying to find by flying against them.

Unlike some later world flights, the route did not skim over the top of the world. Across the Pacific to Japan, the flight plan went down the China coast, west to India, through the Middle East, across Europe and the Atlantic. The route avoided the Soviet Union because the United States did not recognize that government. President Coolidge had told

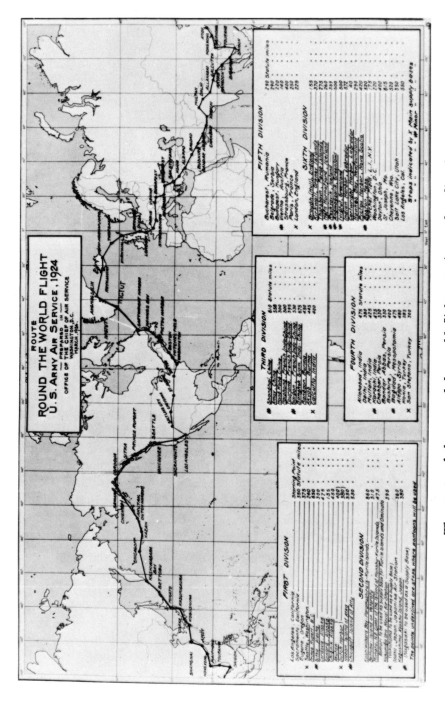

The route of the around-the-world flight, starting and ending in Seattle, Washington.

Congress in December that the United States did not intend to enter into diplomatic relations with a regime that refused to uphold the sanctity of international obligations. The lack of ties with Russia added a few thousand extra miles to make an estimated total of 28,000 miles.

SELECTION OF AN airplane that could withstand extreme conditions was another tough decision. First Lieutenant Erik Nelson, the committee engineering officer, drew up specifications for the aircraft. He had been the engineering officer on the New York to Nome flight, which was now looked upon as their best training experience, and probably knew more about airplane engines than anyone else in the Air Service. Major Hap Arnold, commanding officer at Rockwell Field in San Diego, California, thought Nelson had a natural instinct for diagnosing engine ailments. A native of Sweden, Nelson was a graduate of the Technical University at Stockholm and had spent a number of years at sea before he settled in the United States as a young man. He went to work as an automobile mechanic and later as a motor expert for the Curtiss Aeroplane Company.

When Lt. Colonel James Fechet, the head of the Training and War Plans Division, was commanding officer at Kelly Field, Texas, he wandered into an empty hangar one Saturday morning and found a young man in dirty overalls working on an engine. Surprised to see him working there when almost everyone else had left for the weekend, Fechet asked him who he was and why he was there. Nelson simply replied that he was interested in the engine. The incident made an impression on Fechet and was one reason Nelson received his assignment to the World Flight Committee.

A little known aircraft manufacturer in Santa Monica, California, interested Nelson and he paid him a visit in the summer of 1923. The designer and builder was 32-year-old Donald Douglas. After two years at Annapolis, Douglas had transferred to M.I.T. where, to everyone's surprise, he completed the course in two years. Upon graduation he joined the faculty as an Assistant in Aeronautical Engineering at a salary of $500 a year. He worked with Jerome Clarke Hunsaker on what was probably the first efficient wind tunnel made in America. In this pioneer research, Hunsaker saw the young man's originality, technical competence and persistence. Hunsaker was sure that Douglas would be a leader in aeronautical research; instead, Douglas turned to creative design as an industrialist. In 1915, he worked for the Connecticut Aircraft Company in building the first American dirigible for the United States Navy. Not long after, Glenn Martin, an aircraft manufacturer with a plant in Los Angeles, heard of him and offered him a job as his chief engineer. When the two men met for the first time in a hotel lobby in Los Angeles, Martin was shocked to see that Douglas was only a boy. Young or not, Douglas helped build the Martin Model S, a seaplane that set three world altitude records and held the duration record for three years. Later he designed the prototype of the Martin bomber used by Billy Mitchell in the tests that sank three German warships in 1921.

Douglas, who started his own business in 1920 in the rear of a barber shop, had sold some torpedo planes to the Navy that had impressed Nelson. The offices of the Douglas Company were less impressive. The engineering department, purchasing department and general offices were all contained in one 15′ x 20′ room. The staff, though, included Jack Northrop, later an industry giant, who was one of the company's four engineers in the early days. For a company started only two years earlier on a $600 shoestring, the Douglas company was doing extraordinarily well.

After discussions with Nelson, Arthur Stone and Holzer Wictum, inspectors from the aircraft procurement division of Army Materiel moved into the Douglas offices. Douglas gathered information from the Army and then spent long hours at his drafting board. He based his plans, with many modifications, on his Navy torpedo design. When the plans were completed Nelson received Patrick's approval to go ahead with construction.

Since it was thought that there was safety and success in numbers, four planes were to make up the original complement, with one plane held in reserve. Nelson returned to Santa Monica that summer and worked with Douglas on the details. It has been said that Nelson, the practical flier, and Douglas, the theoretician, argued frequently. They probably did since both were strong-minded sticklers for detail and there were plenty of reasons for different opinions. Despite their battles they respected each other, became good friends and designed an excellent airplane.

When the experimental plane was completed Nelson sent it to

The pilots and mechanics had to pitch in to keep the planes in the air. Here we see Harvey and Martin at work on their Douglas D-WC, the *Seattle*.

McCook Field at Dayton, Ohio for tests and then to Hampton, Virginia for seaplane trials.

The planes, designated D-WC, were sturdy two-place, open-cockpit biplanes capable of carrying a large amount of fuel for long non-stop flights. The maximum fuel capacity was 450 gallons, an insignificant amount when compared to the 48,770-gallon storage of today's 747s that fly non-stop from New York to Tokyo. The oil capacity was 50 gallons. The welded steel tubing fuselage gave greater strength and endurance than the usual wire and wood construction. Varnished linen covered the framework. The wing span was 50 feet and the plane was 35½ feet long. With pontoons the plane weighed about four tons. There were dual controls, an electric starter and the pontoons could be replaced with wheels. Neither sleek nor streamlined, the bull-headed planes gave an appearance of strength.

The two cockpits, one in front of the other, had a stick, or control column, with a control wheel on it. The wheel controlled the ailerons, and moving the column fore and aft controlled the elevators. A bar at the pilot's feet operated the rudder. The plane could be flown from either of the two cockpits. The Army preferred to think of the planes as modified commercial transports rather than modified Navy planes. Both views were correct. Somewhat similar planes had been used commercially on the East Coast. One thing is certain. They were selected to accomplish the purpose of the flight and were not regarded as military aircraft.

The power plant was the latest model 12-cylinder, water-cooled Liberty engine, basically a wartime product. It weighed less than two pounds per horsepower and developed 420 horsepower at full throttle. The plane's rate of climb was a slow 50 feet per minute and its landing speed was 53 miles per hour. The top speed was about 105 miles per hour, but it usually lumbered along at a lot less. Speed is always relative anyway. In the fall of 1923, the air speed record was only 245 miles per hour.

In many ways the statistics of the Douglas planes were less awesome than those of the NC-4 that had crossed the Atlantic five years before. The Navy plane's 126-foot wingspan, four Liberty engines and greater height, weight and space for a crew of six all dwarfed the D-WC. Nevertheless, the World Cruisers were an imposing sight.

There was little doubt about the engines that would be used in the World Cruisers. The Air Service may have been short of airplanes, but they had plenty of engines. In 1924, a surplus of almost 12,000 engines

The D-WC was a big, tough airplane, but it was a very *simple* airplane as this shot of the controls and instrumentation shows.

existed, and in January, Delos Emmons, Chief of Production Engineering at McCook Field, tried to dispose of 5,000 of them. He wrote, "There is no doubt but what the large stock of Liberty engines is hindering engine development." If not obsolete, the Liberty was certainly not an advanced design for a world flight. There were actually a number of engines on the market or in development that were superior in performance. Nevertheless, the Liberty was reliable and lingered on in active use in the Air Service until 1936. During Prohibition days some rumrunners outran the Coast Guard in Liberty-engined speedboats that had been bought from junk dealers.

The Liberty was designed in six jam-packed days at the Willard Hotel in Washington, D.C. Before the war, a total of 666 aircraft had been produced in the United States and only 224 of them were delivered to the Air Service. War made money available for quick results. The question was how to proceed in a limited amount of time.

The Aircraft Production Board, under Colonel E. A. Deeds, later Chairman of the Board of National Cash Register, decided that the United States should design and build a standardized unit of greater horsepower than existing engines that could be produced in quantity. The goal was to meet the opposing requirements of maximum power and minimum weight with economical fuel and oil consumption. The Allies were producing sixty different types of engines that led to high costs, low production and a shortage of parts. European engines, such as the Clerget 130HP, the Rolls-Royce 275HP, the Lorraine Dietrich 270HP or the Bugatti 500HP, could have been produced in the United States, but they were not readily adaptable to American manufacturing methods.

The two Americans who made the engineering decisions were Elbert John Hall and Jesse G. Vincent. Previously unacquainted, they had one thing in common. Both had taught themselves engineering through correspondence courses and were now at the top of their profession. Hall, a Californian, designed and built the Comet automobile and then, with Bert C. Scott, formed the Hall-Scott Motor Car Company to manufacture industrial locomotives, gas-driven railway coaches and interurban car bodies for electric railroads and auto and aviation engines. By 1910 their four- and six-cylinder aviation engines were well known.

Vincent had worked as a machinist and toolmaker and in 1903 was superintendent of inventions for Burroughs Adding Machine Company. Later, he was chief engineer for the Hudson Motor Car Company and then Vice President for engineering at the Packard Motor Car Company. His list of patents was voluminous. Vincent and Hall had gone to Washington in 1917 to sell their respective products to the government when Deeds gave them the common task of designing a practical airplane engine.

The two men went to work in a suite at the Willard Hotel on May 29, 1917. They brought in drafting tables and paper and the next day a volunteer, J. M. Schoonmaker, took over the drawing so that they could dictate a report they had worked on the night before. Since time was critical, they were not interested in developing any new devices. They used their own designs and those of other manufacturers. Nothing was new except the way they put it all together.

Each man contributed a number of features. Hall was responsible for the special method of drawing water from the exhaust side of the cylinder which tended to equalize the heat distribution of the cylinders. The propeller flange drive and the crankshaft were also Hall and Scott designs. The direct-drive feature was one of the main parts that contributed to the success of the engine. Among Vincent's ideas were improved valve action, light steel cylinders, water-jacketed intake headers and two-part box-section crankcases.

On June 1, two layout men came in from Detroit and the five men worked steadily until Monday afternoon, June 4. They completed layouts for longitudinal, transverse and rear elevation, and camshaft assembly views of an eight-cylinder engine. At midnight on the fourth, Hall and Vincent appeared before the joint committee of the Army–Navy Aircraft Production Board, showed the finished drawings, further detailed their plans for the engine and received approval to go ahead. Packard produced the experimental engines in a series that would include four-, six-, eight- and twelve-cylinder engines, each having a four-inch bore and a seven-inch stroke with a maximum of interchangeable parts. The first eight-cylinder Liberty engine was completed 28 days after the drawings had begun.

This was the birth of the Liberty engine which, with modifications, would be used seven years later on the world flight. With typical American energy more than 20,000 engines were produced during the war by such companies as Packard, Lincoln, General Motors and Marmon. Thirty-five engines were taken out of mothballs at Fairfield Air Intermediate Depot and reconditioned. They were fitted with modified cylinders with reinforced heads to lessen the water jacket leaks that had been troublesome in earlier engines. A Delco system with a standard distributor furnished the ignition. The Engineering Division built 31 propellers. Four were sent to Douglas and the remainder to bases scattered around the world. Thirteen were oak propellers to be used with pontoons and 18 were walnut for land use.

Everything did not run smoothly with the new planes. The original four motors supplied to the flight were in poor shape—one motor shipped to Seattle had a faulty shaft assembly that would have certainly broken down before reaching Japan. All of the reconditioned engines were rough and needed many adjustments. Assembling airplane engines in those days seems to have been a slipshod business.

The original plan, later discarded, was to have one plane with a radio. All planes were equipped with brackets and wiring for fast installation if the plane with the radio became disabled. The plan was to install a set with a mean broadcasting radius of 250 miles; one with greater range would weigh too much. Weight, however, finally ruled out all radios, even for the Atlantic crossing.

Weight was a critical problem for the flight and no one knew what would be needed because there were no precedents. Motors could burn out, wings could crumple in rough landings and spark plugs might stop sparking; there were a thousand things that could go wrong and it was anyone's guess what would be needed and where. One officer observed that there were plenty of suggestions about what should be taken along and would have been fine if the plane had the capacity of a freight car. But, unlike Sir Francis Drake, who sailed around the world with his oriental rugs and silver service, the aviators had to watch every ounce that went aboard.

First Lieutenant Elmer Adler was the committee member for supply. He began a pruning process as he wrestled with the conditions that were liable to prevail, the distance between hops and the weight of the fuel. With a useful load per plane of about 5000 pounds, he estimated gasoline at 3600 pounds; crew, 360 pounds; oil, 375 pounds; and water, 84 pounds. The engine would probably consume about 20 gallons of gasoline an hour. Clairvoyance would have been the only sure way to come up with the right answers. Despite not being a clairvoyant, Adler did remarkably well.

The home base for logistics was McCook Field, the center for Army Air Service engineering. Each Division would have a main supply depot and one or more minor depots. The main bases were for motor and

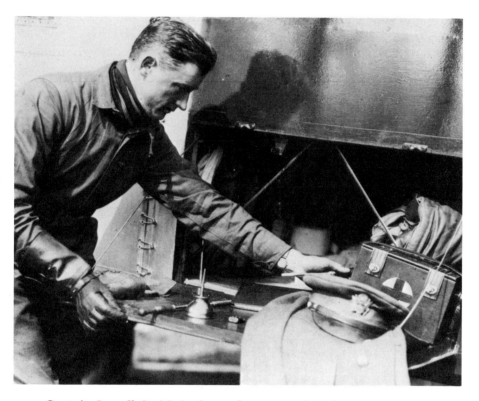

Captain Lowell Smith is shown here arranging the storage space in the fuselage of his plane, the *Chicago*. This is where the crews carried their wardrobes, first aid kits, tools—everything they needed on the trip.

pontoon changes and general overhauls. The minor bases were for replacement of broken or damaged parts. These facilities formed a network spaced about 1500 miles apart. At the earliest possible moment,
emergency engines sufficient for six changes for each plane, 14 sets of
pontoons and 42 landing gears were planted at these stations around the
world. Steamship, rail and often crude local transportation were used
to disperse wings, stabilizers, radiators, engines and a multitude of other
necessities around the world.

The aircraft hardware and smaller parts may have been more troublesome. The relatively simple airplanes of that day required emergency
planning that did not seem so simple. Several hundred items were
needed, ranging from eleven different sizes of flat-head brass wood
screws, four sizes of steel round-head machine screws, cotter pins, lock
washers, castellated nuts and copper and steel tubing to sheet aluminum,
batteries, ignition wire and airplane linen. The list went on and on.

The boxes carrying the supplies were made of ash lumber. This was an
ingenious idea because the wood could be used for emergency parts if
they were caught in a jam. There were also small amounts of spruce
and plywood in each box. Numbered boxes contained exactly the same
equipment wherever deposited. In Alaska or India, the fliers, working
against time, would know immediately where to find the needed part.

Each plane had a specially constructed bag of tools and minor equipment that weighed about 50 pounds. Again there was a question of what
to take and what to leave out. Careful thought went into the kits that
carried hatchets, nails, wrenches, screw drivers, safety wire, turnbuckles,
bolts, calipers, spark plugs, ignition switches, blow torches, glue, gaskets
and patching materials. The pilots made the final decision about the
contents of their own kit. Each plane also carried collapsible water
buckets, oil and gas measures, field glasses, writing pads and thermos
bottles for coffee and concentrated food. They hoped these items would
help in a tight spot, but they couldn't know what, when or where.

The purchase of aircraft, supplies and fuel cost money, a delicate subject in this economy-minded era. Captain William Volandt, a pioneer
in aviation logistics, was the finance member of the committee who had
the thankless task of calculating the costs. He estimated that the total
cost of the flight would be $257,882. An additional sum of $50,000 for
contingency expenses was included in the fiscal 1925 budget. It was
anyone's guess whether or not the American public would get their
money's worth.

III

THE FLIERS

MAJOR GENERAL Patrick knew that the most critical decision of the entire project was the selection of the pilots. The search began for experienced men who could stand the severe mental and physical strain of such a flight. There was also a wariness about candidates who might be distracted by hobnobbing with important personages at the inevitable receptions. A deep feeling permeated the Air Service that the honor of the country was at stake. Commanders of air bases across the country recommended 110 flying officers rated "superior." Four were chosen from this select group, with two alternates.

The Chief took great care in considering the choices for commander of the flight. Among the most prominent names were Hickam, Tinker and Spaatz, future greats of the Air Service. He chose Major Frederick L. Martin. Most members of the Air Staff would have probably selected Spaatz as their first choice. In their eyes, and despite Patrick's flying achievement, Martin had learned to fly too late in life. The general opinion then was that anyone over 25 years of age who took up flying was just too old. Nevertheless, Patrick knew Martin well and had confidence in him.

Martin, a graduate in mechanical engineering from Purdue University, had been in the Army since 1908. During the war he served overseas with the Air Service in supply, became a pilot in 1921 and by 1923 had about 700 flying hours, a respectable amount of experience in the air. At 42, he was the real old man of the group. A married man, he had a six-year-old son. When the call came, he was commanding the Air Service technical school at Chanute Field, Illinois. Distinguished in appearance, articulate and a man of character, he had the rank to give the group stature as they circled the world. Certainly these were among the many factors considered in his selection. It was important to have a proper representative of the United States leading this global mission.

MAJOR HAP ARNOLD, later commander of the Army Air Corps in World War II, wrote a letter recommending First Lieutenant Lowell Smith as his first choice. Smith was one of 40 out-of-luck flying captains who had been demoted in 1922 because of insufficient appropriations for the Air Service. A quiet, 32-year-old Californian, he kept most of his thoughts to himself. What went on behind his gray eyes was often a mystery to his friends.

Hap Arnold had high praise for Smith, and with good reason. Smith had won first place in a transcontinental air race in 1919 and more recently established a new world endurance record of 37 hours, 15 minutes in a de Havilland with his friend, First Lieutenant John Richter. On the same flight, he and Richter were the first men to risk mid-air refueling, a feat often erroneously attributed to Carl Spaatz and his crew in the *Question Mark* six years later. They used a 40 foot, metal lined, flexible 1¼-inch steam hose. One false move, a few drops of gasoline on their hot engine and that would have been the flaming end of both the experiment and the pilots. The better publicized flight of the *Question Mark* actually owed much of its success to the work done by Smith and Richter.

In Arnold's opinion, Smith, who had more than 1500 hours in the air, was one of the best cross-country pilots in the Air Service, and that meant skill at handling the plane, superior mechanical and navigation ability and excellent judgment. Smith had flown from the Canadian border to the Mexican border in 12 hours and 13 minutes with practically no deviation from his scheduled route. After each new record the Flight Surgeon found him in excellent physical condition and showing little sign of mental exhaustion. Smith's record ensured him a slot on the world flight.

Smith's early life had not been easy. His father had given up a good paying job to become an evangelical minister. The idea was that the Lord would provide, but there were days when there was little to eat. Smith had worked at all kinds of jobs, including carnival motorcyclist, yet somehow managed to graduate from San Fernando College. Later, he learned to fly without any trouble because he was extremely well coordinated. For a short time, Smith flew for Pancho Villa while the Mexican rebel tried to take over the presidency of Mexico in 1915 when General Huerta fled the country. Nowadays, Villa is pictured as a bandit and it's forgotten that Woodrow Wilson's administration en-

The full crew turned out for this shot. From left to right they are: Martin, Smith, Wade, Nelson, Harding, Harvey, Ogden and Turner.

couraged his rebellion until the rebel made the fatal error of crossing the Rio Grande and raiding New Mexico.

When World War I started, Smith entered the Air Service where, much to his annoyance, he was kept in the United States as a flying instructor. Finally sent overseas to pilot Handley Page bombers, he arrived in London on Armistice Day. After the war he was an engineer officer at Kelly Field and Rockwell Air Intermediate Depot. From 1919 to 1922 he commanded the 91st Squadron on forest patrol in California, Oregon and Washington. Long flights over vast, trackless forests when his compass was the only means of navigation may have been better training for the world flight than some of his more publicized achievements. Once, on fire patrol, Smith left his heavy deHavilland in the hands of his passenger, a forester who had never flown a plane, climbed far out on the wing, kicked the guard off a radio generator propeller which had been secured by mistake and jumped back into the cockpit. "Had to keep up communications," he explained.

R. L. Walsh, the Commanding Officer at Bolling Field, Anacostia, recommended 28-year-old Leigh Wade, a Michigan native who was known as one of the best pilots in the Air Service. Walsh was confident that he could "hold up under long and severe physical and mental strain." The war had interfered with Wade's ambition to become a doctor. He had not been especially attracted to aviation, but after spending some time in the North Dakota National Guard, including a tour of duty on the Mexican border, he heard that it was a way to win a commission. He trained with the RAF at Toronto, Canada, and received his commission in the United States Army in December 1917. In France, he commanded the 120th Aero Squadron, a service outfit.

The determined Wade had flown all types of planes in all types of weather, had done test work on aerial navigation instruments with the engineering division at McCook Field and had extensive cross country experience. An unexcelled plane handler, he seemed to have an uncanny feel for flying and held an altitude record of more than 27,000 feet in an open cockpit Martin bomber. "It was very cold," he recalled.

When Wade heard the good news about his selection he was sure that someone was pulling his leg. Shortly before he had offered odds that someone from Bolling Field would be chosen and could not find any takers because they had already won more than their share of places in the air races.

The fourth pilot, Erik Nelson, 35, was a natural choice since he was already working on the construction of the planes. A few years before, however, he had been regarded as anything but a natural choice. When World War I began he had the distinction of being rejected once by the Lafayette Escadrille, twice by the RAF and once by the United States Air Service because of age. In October 1917, the Air Service finally accepted him. On the 1920 Alaskan flight he had shown his strength under stress as well as his mechanical ability. Like Wade, he had flown aerial navigation tests.

The friendly, precision-minded Nelson unconsciously attracted stories about himself as a man who could do the impossible. Many of the stories were far-fetched, but they were a sign of respect shown by his fellow fliers. One seemingly far-fetched story was apparently true. During a five and a half hour flight over British Columbia in 1920, Nelson spent part of the time riding astride the fuselage in order to balance a sudden nose heaviness. When the plane came down, the landing gear broke and Nelson catapulted over the top wing. While aghast onlookers feared the worst, he picked himself off the ground unhurt. Part of his popularity came from his captivating smile. People were startled to hear a Swedish accent when he spoke, and were amused at his frequent use of epigrams.

Each pilot was his own man, yet they held certain characteristics in common. Determination, restlessness, energy, mechanical ability and, above all, a love of flying belonged to each of them. The narrow escapes they had all experienced never dampened their enthusiasm. The dignified Martin, the modest Smith, the calm Wade and the precise Nelson were all deceptive men who demanded top performance from themselves and others. And all of them enjoyed the life that they risked every day.

The four pilots and two well qualified alternates, First Lieutenants Leslie Arnold, who had taken part in the bombing tests off the Virginia Capes, and LeClaire Schulze, who won the Pulitzer races in 1923, received orders to Langley Field, Virginia, the first week of 1924 for an intensive training course. Also ordered to the field were several highly recommended aviation mechanics. Each pilot would carefully observe them to pick his flying partner.

The practical course concentrated on the route of the flight. No one wanted to clutter their minds with extraneous facts. Committee mem-

bers reviewed their special studies in detail with the pilots. Bradley
Jones, an aeronautical engineer, taught global navigation because many
maps were inaccurate and much of the route was over water. Major
William Blair of the Signal Corps taught meteorology. There was a lot
to learn about flying weather and few people knew much about the
subject. Major Herbert Neblett lectured on medicine, and Erik Nelson
brought the men up to date on his tests with the airplane. There was
also survival work, engineering maintenance, checking and double
checking the flight plan and making necessary modifications to the plans
and the planes.

Each afternoon, after class, they went over scads of maps in a room
they had taken over in the Officer's Club, or tested the prototype
Douglas cruiser. A Navy commander named DeWitt C. Ramsey
helped them with float-plane configurations that were new to them.
They also carried test loads up to a total weight of 8300 pounds to determine the most suitable pontoons and propellers for heavy-duty work
and to spot any weaknesses during continuous service. Their findings
were sent to Douglas, who incorporated changes in constructing the
four planes to be used on the flight. It was a good system that they believed worked out well.

At the end of six weeks training the pilots studied all the large-scale
maps for the entire route, marked lines of flight, filled in distance and
compass courses and noted emergency harbor facilities and landing
fields. Then they shipped the maps to the main supply base for each
Division around the world to await their arrival.

The pilots selected their mechanics, called "mechanicians," before
leaving for Santa Monica. Martin chose Staff Sergeant Alva Harvey,
23 years old, of Cleburne, Texas, a five-year Army veteran. Martin
sized up the modest, gentlemanly Harvey as a young man with will
power plus mechanical ability. Smith selected Technical Sergeant
Arthur Turner, who had been in charge of mechanical work for the
forest patrol aircraft on the Pacific coast. Wade's pick was Staff Sergeant Henry Ogden of Woodville, Mississippi, another 23-year-old,
who had served as an instructor in aviation mechanics.

The Chief of Air Service gave permission to select one officer as a
mechanic "if the flight so desired." The flight did indeed so desire.
There was only one trouble. Martin, at Nelson's instigation, requested
a civilian with a reserve commission. The War Department rejected

the request with the statement that all officers on the flight should be regular Army. Martin persisted, however, and Second Lieutenant John Harding, 27, joined the group.

During the war Harding had attended the Air Service Mechanics School and had risen to Master Sergeant with a rating of Master Signal Electrician and Aviation Mechanician. A native of Nashville, Tennessee, he was a member of the prominent family that once owned Belle Meade, a famous plantation of 5500 acres that bred the ancestors of famous thoroughbreds Secretariat and Seattle Slew. He had a natural bent for mechanics and had studied mechanical engineering at Vanderbilt University. Before the war he had worked for the Chalmers Motor Car Company and Dodge. The handsome Harding had an unusual distinction. He had one blue and one brown eye.

In 1919, Harding had impressed Lieutenant Harmon, who had taken him along as mechanic on the "round the rim" of the United States flight. Nelson had also worked with Harding and he knew his man. It was a tribute to Harding that Nelson, a hard taskmaster, requested this easy-going mechanic. It was also a clue to Harding's inner strength. Beneath the smiling, happy-go-lucky exterior was a first-rate mechanical mind and a spirit that could endure pressure.

BEFORE THE NEW team took the train to California, introductions to the Secretary of War and President of the United States were necessary formalities. First, Patrick took them to meet the Secretary of War. After a 40 minute wait, Weeks burst in and exclaimed, "Who are these people?" An explanation followed and then they dashed over to the White House and waited there for an hour. Finally, after the President met a group of farmers and some American Indians, and no one else was in the anteroom, they were ushered in to see President Coolidge in the green carpeted Oval Office.

Contrary to impressions given by some historians, the President was a busy man. Wade noticed the pile of papers on his desk and realized that he was pressed for time. Arnold, one of the alternate pilots, thought that the President had a neat way of doing things. As he approached Coolidge there was an open door just beyond. The President stood on the left side of the door and a Secret Service man on the right side. As Arnold extended his right hand and gave a slight bow, the President gave a little tug to pull him off balance so that the Secret Service man could guide him out almost before he knew what happened.

Someone suggested that a picture of the President with the fliers would be good publicity. It was a Presidential election year. They lined up in the garden with an empty spot in the middle for the President. He came out saying, "Hurry up, hurry up." The send-off was not the most heartwarming, but Wade, less critical than Arnold, thought that at least the President gave them a pleasant smile.

The pilots and mechanics started work the day they arrived at the Douglas factory in Santa Monica and they lived with the planes until they were completed. Nelson made several flight tests in plane number one that resulted in minor changes in all planes to increase stability. When the planes rolled off the line one by one, the assigned pilots flew them to Rockwell Field at San Diego for a shakedown cruise and final touches such as varnishing, swinging compasses and arranging racks for tools, spare parts and map containers. Before they finished, however, they changed all motors because of a lack of rpm. Hours meant nothing to them. When Harding discovered that the engine on his plane was rough and noisy, he worked until three the next morning replacing it.

Everyone was anxious to get started. On March 17, after some deliberations about the weather, three planes departed from Clover Field near Los Angeles. Nelson's plane had not been delivered and would join them in Seattle, the official starting place. Crowds in horse-drawn carriages, automobiles and on foot watched the planes warm up. The curious crowd could not escape a sense of enthrallment as they watched the fliers quietly work around the large planes.

No one could minimize the courage of these men. Anything might happen to them in the coming weeks and the unmentionable thought of death lurked in the back of everyone's mind as they shared the excitement of the imminent adventure.

At 9:30 A.M. the planes took off in a cyclone of red dust. Unofficially, at least, the world flight had begun. The three planes flew over mountains and low clouds to the excellent flying country over the Sacramento Valley. This was territory that Smith knew like the back of his hand. Martin made a brief stop at Lake Merced to make some minor adjustments, but everything seemed to be going smoothly and all arrived at Sacramento in the early afternoon. They averaged about 80 miles an hour.

PREDICTIONS FOR THE flight ranged from dark pessimism to sheer bravado. In a burst of overoptimistic national pride, a *New York Times* editorial claimed that with good luck the flight should be accomplished in not much more than 30 days. At worst, "If the start is made in early April, Americans should make the greatest of her aeronautical records by the Fourth of July, allowing for all mischances and delays." The proposed British flight with one machine and meager preparations was looked upon as a mere sporting event, while the American flight was called a scientific plan to promote commercial aviation.

Such a schedule was beyond the wildest dreams of the American airmen. More realistically, Martin said that they had prepared for a five and a half month schedule and with luck they might be back in the United States a month ahead of time. A long expedition was ahead of them, not an overnight sensation.

In the next two days they hopped to Eugene, Oregon, and then to Vancouver, Washington. The weather was excellent. In the afternoon of the second day, heavy rain and fog forced them back and delayed their arrival in Seattle until the following day. Nelson was not too happy about being left behind in Los Angeles. Two days later, eager to catch up, he made one non-stop flight of 800 miles from Santa Monica to Eugene, and another non-stop jump to Seattle, arriving only a few hours after the first three planes.

At Seattle the seemingly endless preparations began again. Planes one, three and four were varnished, and plane three had a new motor installed. Pontoons replaced wheels on all aircraft, anchors and ropes were fitted for emergency use, and the "very final" selection of tools and spare parts were made with careful attention to total weight. Actually, the preparations *were* endless and would not be completed until the flight was over. Harding wrote in his diary, "Just work-work-work—Barrels of work." At the last moment before departure the employees of the small Boeing Aircraft Company, previously a manufacturer of wood products, came to the rescue by working through the night to repair damage to the metal tip on the propeller of Martin's plane.

While in Seattle, an unexpected complication developed. It was found that Turner had a lung condition that disqualified him from continuing the flight. Smith now had a fast decision to make. Who should replace Turner? Time was an important element and Smith, after some heavy thinking, concluded that on such short notice it would be wiser to select one of the fully briefed alternate pilots. He chose Arnold.

Good-natured Leslie Arnold, 29 years old, well qualified as both pilot and mechanic, was astonished to hear the news. Smith asked him if he would work like the devil. He answered, "Sure, I'll work like a whole flock of devils."

Arnold had worked on submarines in New London, Connecticut, until one day in 1917 he read that the Army needed aviators and decided that was the field for him. He reached the front in France three days before the end of the war and remained with the veteran First Aero Squadron until ordered home in July 1919. In 1921, during the bombing tests that sank the German battleship *Ostfriesland* off the Virginia Capes, he served as "sort of an aide" to Billy Mitchell. Although he did not know for sure, he always suspected that Mitchell, who he said you either loved or hated, had something to do with his original consideration for the flight. A onetime actor in summer stock who had played in *Brewster's Millions* and *The House of a Thousand Candles*, Arnold's outgoing personality was the opposite of Smith's and they made a well-balanced pair.

WITH THE DATE of departure near, the four planes were christened for American cities. Since they were in the Prohibition era of the Eighteenth Amendment, bottles of water replaced champagne. Ingenuity allegedly came to the fore with water from Lake Washington for Martin's plane, number one, which became the *Seattle*. Water from Lake Michigan doused Smith's plane, number two, which became the *Chicago*. The Atlantic Ocean supplied water for Wade's plane, number three, which became the *Boston*, and the Gulf of

Mexico helped transform Nelson's plane, number four, into the *New Orleans*. No section of the country could complain about not being represented.

As the starting time drew near, there was some news from overseas. European newspapers haughtily claimed that Americans were good at racing and stunt flying, but did not produce long-distance aircraft, and foreign nations were not averse to making unflattering comparisons between their own machines and semi-official aircraft industries and the fledgling Douglas D-WC. It made good advertising.

Near the end of March, Squadron Leader A. Stuart MacLaren, a distinguished British war pilot, and two companions, Flying Officer W. A. Plenderleith and Sergeant R. Andrews, were ready to take off in a Vickers amphibian powered by a 450HP Napier Lyon engine. MacLaren, an Oxfordshire man, conceived the idea for a world flight in 1922, but political unrest in Constantinople had blocked passage to the Middle East and he reluctantly postponed his plans. In many ways, the British team was the best qualified for a world flight. All of the crew had seen action in the air in World War I and had worked together in the Middle East after the war. MacLaren had won the Military Cross for conspicuous gallantry, a bar to the cross, the Distinguished Flying Cross and an Air Force Cross. Now 32 years old, he was another of the modest breed of airmen who were as skillful as they were courageous. When asked about his decorations, he usually answered in his most understated British style that it was simply for "Shoving down a few Hun planes and odd things."

Plenderleith had also been mentioned in war despatches. While a pilot in Number 54 Squadron he was badly wounded in a battle with a superior number of German planes while over the enemy lines. Somehow he managed to return to base and was later assigned to the defense of London where he did considerable night flying.

MacLaren had actually flown from England to India in a Handley Page in 1918. It was an invaluable experience on a large chunk of the route of his proposed world flight. Familiarity with landing areas in far off places gave him a distinct advantage over the Americans.

MacLaren was to be the navigator, Plenderleith the pilot and Andrews the mechanic. When the flight reached Tokyo, the British planned to jettison a 250-pound undercarriage and take on a fourth crew member, Lt. Colonel L. E. Broome, a mining engineer who was well-acquainted with the North Pacific. Two years before he had worked on plans for an airway there. Until they arrived, he served as an advance officer.

MacLaren's flight was not an official mission of the RAF. He was placed on half pay for the duration and merely had the best wishes of British air leaders. Confident of success, he offered to race the Americans, but Patrick turned down the opportunity and said they had no intention of speeding up. That was the official reply, but whether or not he accepted the challenge, everyone knew that the race was on.

IV

ALASKA AND
THE ALEUTIANS

CIRCLING OVER Seattle on April 6, 1924, Arnold thought of the local newspaper that hinted there was not much hope they would complete their journey. There were plenty of reasons to believe the paper. No one had ever flown across the Pacific and only the British dirigible R-34 had crossed the Atlantic from east to west. Still, the world flight was on its way. Arnold had no doubts about himself as he wondered who else would make it.

The bulky planes clearly identified their purpose on both sides of the fuselage with a large insignia. It was a round world showing the western hemisphere surrounded by a cloud of light blue-gray. Above the world in chrome yellow letters edged with black were the words, "Air Service, USA," and below the world, "World Flight." Two eagles painted in natural color flew towards the center from each side. The forward part of the plane itself was aluminum in color. Aft of the rear cockpit was a blend of chocolate brown and olive green.

When the planes reached Port Townsend, about 45 miles from Seattle, Martin discovered that Wade was not with them. A photographic plane had previously obscured his view. Since all planes carried a maximum amount of gasoline, Martin decided that it would be unsafe to land with all that weight in order to find out what happened to him. Disturbed, they continued on the way to Prince Rupert, British Columbia, Canada.

They flew north from Puget Sound, over the Strait of Georgia to Queen Charlotte Sound, where fog forced them close to the water. The glassy water made it almost impossible for them to estimate their altitude. Reaching open sea, they flew over rough waves that from the air looked about 40 feet high. It was great sport to watch them dash against the shore; greater yet, Arnold thought, to imagine a forced landing. The weather was squally and as they approached Prince Rupert a heavy snowstorm raged. Rain changed to sleet and sleet to snow. Nelson, flying on one side of the triangular formation, could not see Smith on the other side. The mayor claimed it was the worst day in ten years and the newspapermen had gone home not expecting anyone to show up.

Martin, blinded by the storm, knew that there was a sawmill on his right, a hill ahead and a mountain on his left, so he stalled the plane to check his speed for a pancake landing. About ten feet above the water the forward speed vanished and the heavy plane dropped. He struck the surface with such force the two outer wing struts holding the upper and lower wings apart on the left side broke in two and four vertical brace wires snapped. The ship rattled as though it had received a death blow and it looked like a total wreck. Martin's first thought was that there would be nothing left but kindling wood. To his surprise, a careful inspection showed that the damage was less than expected. Nevertheless, it was enough to cause a delay.

Thirty-five minutes after the three planes landed, the missing Wade showed up. His heavily loaded plane had held up his takeoff for an hour and ten minutes. Once off the water, he took the "Inside Passage" and improved the flying time of the others by 35 minutes.

Spare parts on board the planes and two new struts made in the machine shop of a Canadian drydock took care of the damaged *Seattle*. Already the work of the advance officer was paying off. The next day, while Martin and Harvey worked on their plane, Harding enjoyed a lunch of steamer clams, cheese, crackers and ten percent lager beer supplied by an old salt who guarded his plane and had a houseboat nearby.

On April 10, the flight took off for Sitka in good style. Flying over barren inlets, sounds and channels, often with hills on each side, they continually checked their large-scale maps, which were cut in strips and rolled for easy handling, and kept a sharp lookout. Each wished he had more than two eyes. Hundreds of logs floated in the narrows, so an emergency landing was out of the question. Crossing the 25 mile stretch of Christian Sound the planes bounced like corks. The swells were eight to ten feet high, visibility was 100 yards, and their altitude was 20 or 30 feet. While they were out of sight of land, Harding silently talked to his plane's motor. One happy sight was the appearance of two fishing smacks about halfway across. All hands were on deck waving frantically and the fliers appreciated the friendly greeting. When they stood up in the cockpit to wave back, the rain drops felt like lead shot hitting their faces and hands. Cold as it was, they did not wear gloves because it was too difficult to continually clean goggles and make note of times on maps with their hands covered. Passing over Ketchikan, they saw that the whole town was on the docks waving to them. Forced to fly low because of the fog, they were only about 200 feet above.

When they reached Baranoff Island, they made their way to Sitka and circled once to look it over. It was a picturesque place and Martin thought the fir trees surrounding the harbor shone like emeralds on a sapphire background. After landing, Arnold and Ogden made a mad dash ashore to claim the honor of the first to set foot in Alaska. Ogden won by inches. Worn out, they still had lots of work ahead of them.

People wondered what kept them so busy after a hop. That was easy to answer. The planes' routine maintenance took a tremendous amount of time. Tired or not, they checked the oil, gasoline and water and filled the tanks for the next jump. Then they washed down the engine and body, selected personal baggage to take to their quarters, including thermos bottles, cameras, films and maps. They also covered the engine and cockpits, checked the ignition, rigging wires and pontoons, flushed gasoline strainers, cleaned the voltage regulator and reversed the current relay coil breaker gaps. In cold climates they filled the radiators with a mixture of alcohol, glycerine and water. That was just the routine maintenance; if anything sounded wrong or felt strange they had to work until they figured out the problem.

While the men worked at Sitka, Indians from the Jackson Mission School rowed out to see the planes. It was a new experience for them as they watched in total silence. Martin was impressed by their quiet manner. Back in the States, they would have been flooded with questions.

At Sitka, where rain or snow fell more than 200 days a year and most of the other days were cloudy, the greatest danger came after they landed. A strong southwest wind blew the *Boston* and its 500-pound concrete block anchor almost into the *New Orleans*. Two planes could have been lost then and there. Another time the *New Orleans* slipped its shackle and broke loose from its mooring. Harding was on board when the plane started to drift. What should he do? No one was nearby to help and a dozen questions rushed through his mind. How much time did he have? Should he start the covered engine and risk a fire? Did he have time to take the cover off? Should he wait for a launch to throw him a line? In the direction he was drifting he saw nothing except a jagged, rocky shore so, acting on impulse, he uncovered the engine and cockpit covers and tried the starter. Nothing happened.

He tried again. To his relief it worked. If it had failed the *New Orleans* would have ended up on the rocks. With the plane under control, he taxied to the buoy and once again made fast.

Most of one day was spent tossing around in small boats trying to prevent collisions. When the planes were finally double anchored everyone was soaking wet, cold, tired and hungry. Eighteenth Amendment or not, they cracked open the medical supply and had a good stiff drink. Being wet and cold would become a habit before Alaska was behind them. There would be other times when they tapped the gallon of pure alcohol for the cooling system in Box One to make a hot toddy. These dramatic little episodes sound amusing in the retelling, but they were a great strain on the men. They occurred continually and no one knew at what minute of the day or night their plane might be destroyed and force them out of the flight. Time and again they rushed out with their hearts in their mouths to barely avert disaster and end up frozen with boots full of salt water.

ON THE 13th, Wade took his turn in the lead as the four planes worked their way up the coast to Seward. In and out of bad weather, there were times when they flew along the beach no more than 100 feet above the breakers that were their only visible navigation aids. The Pacific was on their left, timberlands on their right. Nelson stood up in the cockpit with his feet on the rudder-bar so that he could look over the front and side to see the beach. Every few minutes the melting snow blurred his goggles and he had to change them. Once, Wade suddenly turned to avoid striking the irregular shoreline head on and the others, almost on top of him, swerved quickly to avoid a mid-air collision. Flying in formation was ticklish business, especially since they did not wear parachutes. Sometimes the only way they could tell a plane was ahead of them in the fog was when they started to bump from the prop wash.

About ten o'clock there was clear weather for awhile that gave them a good view of the Brady Glacier to the southeast of Icy Point. Square miles of ice stacked hundreds of feet in the air without a sign of life was a lonesome, eerie sight. Shortly after noon, snow-capped mountains of 12,000 to 17,000 feet appeared on the right and a solid wall of dark snow clouds ahead of them looked impenetrable. They went down to ten feet above the shore for the next half hour until they came out of it near the Bering Glacier. All four planes bunched together and rough air almost made them touch wings. Harding was sure that at times the pontoons were not five feet from the surf. Fortunately, the beach was sandy and straight.

Too close to each other for too long, the pilots decided to spread out before their luck gave way. Nelson slowed down and let Wade and Martin pull ahead. To the rear was Smith. By the time they came out of the fog they had lost sight of each other. Harding, wondering about the fate of the others looked around. "Believe me," he wrote, "it looked good to see two little spots way ahead on the horizon and later see No. 2 come out of the mist to the rear and quite a distance back for safety. Well, was tough, so nuf sed." Now flying conditions were good except for strong head winds. Although revving 1600 rpm, it took them two hours and ten minutes to do one stretch of 150 miles. At 4:09 P.M., after seven hours and forty-four minutes in the air, they landed in the calm waters of Seward's Resurrection Bay, thankful that the worst leg so far was over. Seward, at the north end of the bay on Kenai Peninsula, was the southern terminal for a government railroad that ran to Anchorage and was also a port for fishing smacks. The landlocked bay gave good protection.

WEATHER WAS NOT the only danger. Heading for Chignik, a small village on the southeastern shore of the long Alaskan Peninsula, the air was luminous, a light wind blew and the day became beautiful. Nelson took his turn as flight leader. He flew at 1000 feet. Martin was on his left, about 300 yards to the rear. Wade and Smith were on the right at an altitude of about 500 feet. According to plan, canneries along the way with radio equipment reported the time the planes passed over to the Dutch Harbor station. Suddenly, off Cape Igvak, Harvey noticed that the *Seattle* had no oil pressure. Martin quickly throttled down to save the engine and glided to the lee side of the cape. As they glided down, Harvey climbed out on the wing to see if the trouble could be corrected in the air but found the side of the ship covered with oil. On landing he found a hole in the crankcase that he could put his fist through. The others watched the *Seattle* drop back and swing towards Portage Bay. They did not know whether Martin was in difficulty or following in the rear.

It was 2:40 P.M. and Martin was sure that the others had seen him and Harvey go down. He expected them to return in about three hours or as soon as they could refuel at Chignik, 100 miles away. By 6:15 P.M. that hope vanished. Snow came down intermittently and they were extremely uncomfortable. For supper each had five malted tablets. At least they were well dressed for the weather. All the fliers wore flannel shirts, heavy breeches and fur-lined gabardine jerkins. Drawn over that was a one-piece suit of gabardine cloth lined with silk.

Martin told Harvey that he intended to remain with the ship but there were dangers and he did not want him to do anything he considered unwise. The starter had broken and they would be helpless if the anchor dragged. Harvey simply answered, "I am going to stay with you." Together they stood watches, catnapped and waited in misery through the night. The tall men had no room to stretch their legs in the small cockpit. It could have been worse. April 15 and 16 were the only good days in the vicinity in eight months. Nearby Kanatak was a storm center of the Alaskan Peninsula known as the Cauldron of Winds.

At Chignik, the radio station that had been set up by Bissell went to work. Sergeant Rogers had come to Chignik several weeks before to set up his equipment and report weather for the flight. Radio was still a novelty and the efficient Rogers fascinated the fliers by talking with his key to stations hundreds of miles away. Requests went out to two destroyers that had been taking soundings for a new submarine cable between Seattle and Seward to proceed to the vicinity of Portage Bay where the *Seattle* was last seen. The Navy wasted no time. The *Hull* and the *Corey* rushed to the area at full speed, covering 312 miles at a rate of 31 knots. Broadcasts also alerted other vessels nearby.

Bissell and Blair, the weather observer, were on board the Coast Guard Cutter *Haida* and kept their radio officer, Ensign Lee Baker, busy. Listening for news of the downed fliers was everyone's chief occupation. The thought of an engine failure haunted the minds of all the fliers since they knew that it could happen to any one of them at any time.

At 4:45 the next morning, Martin saw wisps of smoke on the horizon. Ships came into view and he fired a white rocket from a Very pistol, followed by two more at one minute intervals. As the ships moved away, Martin desperately fired three red rockets. There was no response. The destroyer *Hull* came into the east side of the bay some distance away, dropped anchor and remained there until 9:00 A.M. Sighting a plane riding low in the water on a gray day was a tough assignment, but finally the ship turned in the direction of the *Seattle* and sent a launch to tow the plane astern. The crew of the *Hull* was jubilant. They had beaten the *Corey* even though it had gone to White Bay, where the chance of finding the fliers seemed better. Suffering from exposure, Martin and Harvey were taken to nearby Kanatak where the Coast Guard Cutter *Algonquin* rushed a new engine from Dutch Harbor. It also carried 300 gallons of gasoline, 20 gallons of lubricating oil and ten boxes of accessories.

Wisely, the planners had asked for the help of the Coast Guard early in the year. To do otherwise would have been foolhardy since no one knew this part of the world better than the sturdy Coast Guardsmen. Rear Admiral F. C. Billard, the Commandant, offered full support and issued orders to the Commander of the Bering Sea Patrol to cooperate in every possible way. With or without orders, the Coast Guard always answered calls for help, but they gladly assumed this extra duty even as they performed just about every imaginable function in these northern waters. Here, the Coast Guard delivered mail, watched over native villages, gave medical care and even served as judges.

When news reached Washington that the planes had become separated, the jumpy General Staff was not pleased. The whole idea of using four planes was for them to stick together for safety. Major General Hines, the Deputy Chief of Staff, directed Patrick to instruct the fliers to remain within sight of one another. Perhaps, too, the Army General Staff wanted to show its authority since Billy Mitchell was not making the Air Service too popular with them these days. He had once confided in his diary that, "The General Staff is now trying to run the Air Service with just as much knowledge of it as a hog knows about skating." Nevertheless, the order, which was undoubtedly sensible, was easier said in Washington than done in Alaska. The other three pilots were flying into increasingly heavy winds and did not have enough fuel to investigate and still reach Chignik.

THE THREE PLANES at Chignik were ready to continue on the 18th, but radio reports arrived from the west that snow, rain and fog were all along the route. To remain on the ground was an easy decision that day. They had already experienced enough thrills from overanxiety to push ahead. Harding wrote,

> The people back home I'm sure are wondering "why don't they go ahead?" Well here's some of the reasons—who wants to or could fly 300 to 500 miles over deep blue seas, rough jagged desolate rocks and snow covered mountains through rain, fog and snow, knowing that there are no signs of civilization in hundreds of miles of you if the old engine should go bye-bye? T'isnt so nice anyway so with good or fair weather we'll continue. We realize we are going slow but why not play the cards right if success is desired? We'll do our best and that's all any man can do.

From the start they had known the odds against them and decided that all they could do was their best. It became a mental refrain that they continually repeated to themselves.

The next morning they were up early, checking the oil and scurrying around before takeoff. Harding thought that the Alaskan surroundings did not exactly help some of their dispositions. He thought he received more than his share of abrupt orders but if anyone could take things in stride it was Harding. He convinced himself that no one really meant to be gruff.

On the flight to Dutch Harbor they took some of their worst jolts in the air. The noses went up and down and the wings batted up, down and sideways. The pilots' wheels spun in both directions and the rudder-bars swung from side to side to keep the planes upright. Fortunately, their engines kept humming. On one stretch the wind was square on the nose. The air speed was 80 to 85 miles per hour while the ground speed was 58 miles per hour. The mechanics, drenched with water from lying flat on the pontoons to release the moorings at Chignik, were just about solid ice by the time they reached Dutch Harbor. How they kept healthy is a mystery. It was a long, hard seven hours and twenty-six minutes to make only 390 miles. They arrived tired, disagreeable and hungry. Resilience, however, was one of their attributes. A turkey dinner on board the *Haida* improved their spirits.

When a gale cleared sufficiently to work on the engine of the *Seattle* at Kanatak, Martin was in bed on the verge of pneumonia. Harvey, with the help of a machinist's mate from the *Algonquin*, started at 7:30 in the evening to replace the engine and worked all night under the light of three gas lanterns. The temperature ranged down to 16° Fahrenheit, snow fell and much of the work was done without gloves. The men must have suffered miserably, but Martin said that Harvey never complained and treated it as routine.

There seemed to be no limit to the help that the men on the *Algonquin* gladly gave. They admired the courage of the fliers and being a part of the world flight pleased them. No hardship was too much in lending a hand. By the 25th, while the thermometer hovered around zero, a working party of twelve men from the Coast Guard ship under Lt.(jg) O'Neill had broken enough of the ice around the plane to move the plane about 500 yards. Then the tide fell so rapidly that the pontoons would no longer float. Nothing came easily. It was impossible to lift the plane bodily, so the men collected all the lumber they could find, built a large sled under the pontoons and had a Standard Oil tractor haul the plane down the creek. When the sides of the ravine became too narrow for the plane to pass they dug out the sides. Nothing stopped them. Late in the morning the plane floated and Martin hopped off in the eye of a strong southeast wind and heavy snow with visibility about 1000 yards. If he had waited the aircraft would have been dashed to pieces by the breakers. In Martin's opinion, no plane had ever taken off in such rough water.

Once in the air, the aileron controls were stiff, probably because the snow had melted and then frozen on the control cables. It took all of Martin's strength to maneuver and he was soon perspiring despite the cold. Weaving his way through thick snow, he saw a lagoon near Portage Bay and thought about landing. He signaled to Harvey who shook his head against the idea. By now Martin respected Harvey's instinct for danger and he kept going. Flying at an altitude of about 100 feet above the water, Martin kept his eyes glued on the shoreline while Harvey kept watch on the opposite side. The indented coast could easily trap them. Martin suddenly felt a vicious kick of the rudder. Harvey had spotted a mountain on their left side only 100 yards away. Martin took a quick look, banked the plane vertically and swung it about on its beam ends. It was a desperate risk so close to the water that the slightest slip would crash them into the sea, but the only other choice was crashing into the mountain. The heavy ship turned and headed out into the storm and continued in and out, back and forth, dodging islands until after what seemed an eternity, it reached Chignik.

At Chignik, a native village with a half dozen houses and a few huts, the *Seattle* was held down by furious gales that were unprecedented for that time of year. The temperature ranged from a warm 60° to a cold 25° Fahrenheit and the winds made 180° shifts. One day over 400 pounds of ice formed on the *Seattle* and it looked like it was made of spun glass. On the 29th, the *Algonquin* anchored off Seal Cape in 16 fathoms of water with 105 fathoms on both chains to ride out a northwest storm with winds blowing up to 70 miles per hour.

SMITH, WADE AND Nelson had troubles of their own while they waited for Martin at Dutch Harbor, one of the few good harbors in the Aleutians and the main depot for the First Division. Wade's engine had developed a distinct bearing knock that sounded to Nelson as though something was going to jump out of the plane at any instant. Despite special anchors, drifting in the rough sea continued and they were forced to beach the planes on a temporary runway. With the help of two booms from a friendly freighter, the *Boston* received a new motor and minor repairs were made to the *Chicago* and *New Orleans*.

One day, Arnold attempted to wash the wings and the hot water froze before he could rinse off. Ogden, following Wade's orders, tried to varnish the pontoons. He heated the varnish in a pail of hot water and it ended up like cold glue. He surrendered too. Actually, the men were surprised that the planes had withstood all of the punishment so well. Rocked, twisted and thrown about in rain, sleet, snow and gusts, they had survived. No one had expected that they would receive such harsh treatment.

With their work finished, time hung heavily on their hands. While waiting in their bunkhouse, they listened to local fishermen, mostly Russians and Swedes, tell wild tales about bear hunts and sea lions. The airmen decided that if half the stories were true the fishermen led exciting lives. Sometimes, when they tired of tall stories, they read; sometimes they played acey-deucy. One night, on the eve of Russian Easter, they all went to a midnight service at the Orthodox Catholic Church. None of them understood the four-hour service, but the candlelight, robes and incense impressed them. Even more impressive were the children in the church who wore their thin white vestments without shivering.

For two days the "woolies" or "williwaws" tore around from almost any direction at unforeseen times without any apparent reason. They upset rowboats, blew planks from the dock and picked up sheets of water and carried them down the bay. Nerves were on edge. Each pilot had his own way of doing things and sometimes when their opinions differed tempers flared. Wade, something of an amateur psychologist, kept the peace as much as anyone in these dismal days and they decided to agree to a spirit of "one for all, and all for one." Nevertheless, waiting was a curse. They realized that despite all of their planning the flight was off to a bad start.

Martin, impatient himself, could easily imagine the impatience of the others waiting for him. Reporting his situation to Smith, the next in command, he ended one message, "Don't get restless—fighting hard to join you."

NERVES WERE TAUT in Washington, too. Tough-minded Lt. Colonel J. E. Fechet, Chief of Training and War Plans, wrote Patrick that the British world flight had reached Karachi in a month while the Air Service had covered far fewer miles in 39 days. Fechet was a planner who hated paperwork. He wanted action. If the British completed their flight with one plane and sketchy preparations he was sure it would detract from the prestige of American aviation. He raised a basic question in his memorandum: Should the planes wait for Martin or proceed without him?

Perhaps the Americans should have been even more concerned

about a young Frenchman who was speeding across Europe and through the Middle East on his way to Tokyo. Lieutenant Pelletier d'Oisy and his mechanic, Bernard Vésin, had taken off from Villacoublay Aerodrome on April 24 in an ordinary Breguet military biplane bearing the badge of the Tunisian Squadron, a black cat mewing at a crescent moon. He made a non-stop flight of 1240 miles to Bucharest in eleven hours, and in four hops reached Basra, Iraq, a distance of 2800 miles, in three days. His 370HP Lorraine-Dietrich engine hummed along perfectly.

The *London Times* regarded d'Oisy's flight as a quick reaction to the British and American world flights intended to maintain French aeronautical prestige. The French were proud of their aeronautical achievements and sensitive to threats to their world leadership. After all, they were among the first to build engines specifically for aircraft, and Louis Bleriot was the first to fly across the English Channel. The daring d'Oisy's arrangements, sparse at best, had been kept secret until the last moment. A rugged six-footer, he was a well known rugby player before the war. During the war he had won many decorations as a flier and the previous year he had made an impressive non-stop flight from Tunis to Paris.

The Portuguese were doing well too. Captain Brito Paes and Lieutenant Sarmento Beires had taken off from Amadoro, near Lisbon, in the Breguet plane, *Patria*, and had reached Bushire, Persia, by April 30.

NOTHING SEEMED TO go right for the Americans. Martin anxiously took off for Dutch Harbor on the 30th during a lull in a storm. Hours passed and he did not arrive. The *Haida* and the Dutch Harbor base listened for news of Martin from cannery stations along the route. The only report was from Chignik telling that the *Seattle* had left. That meant Martin had not passed the first reporting station and must be down between Chignik and King Cove. Waiting and hoping during the dark night, the *Haida* turned on a big searchlight and played it across the sky to act as a guide. The *Algonquin* searched coves along the rocky coast.

The *Algonquin* requested canneries in Chignik Bay to send boats westward to search. Their message was sent all the way to Kodiak to relay to Chignik because they could not reach Sergeant Rogers. They had tried all day to contact Rogers without success, and then finally heard him sending press to Kodiak and signing off, "Good night, I will not be on until 11:00 A.M. tomorrow." Rogers may have had his reasons, but this was beyond the comprehension of the men on the *Algonquin*. The commanding officer, Cecil Gabbett, showed his dismay in his report. He could not understand shutting down when no word had been received that Martin had landed safely. When the cutter signaled "no trace" the hunt intensified.

For three days, heavy radio traffic poured in and out of the *Haida*. A deluge of false reports, reports with no news, directions, orders and suggestions arrived. The main transmitting set on the *Haida* was a two-kilowatt arc that operated better on high wavelengths that reached Vancouver than on low wavelengths. So the radio operator used an auxiliary half-kilowatt spark set with ten amperes radiation because of the difficulties with the larger transmitter.

Patrick received a reassuring message from Smith that gave no information except between the lines. It was obvious that there was no news and no basis for optimism. Some thought the flight should be called off. Instead, Patrick, in no mood to give up, telegraphed Smith:

DO NOT DELAY LONGER WAITING FOR MAJOR MARTIN TO JOIN YOU STOP SEE EVERYTHING DONE POSSIBLE TO FIND HIM STOP PLANES NUMBER 2, 3 AND 4 PROCEED TO JAPAN AT EARLIEST POSSIBLE MOMENT.

On May 3, the flight was up at daylight and with the help of natives the three planes were launched. Smith led the way to the little village of Nazan, on Atka, where Major Blair, the Signal Corps meteorologist, had set up a temporary weather station. Blair was a big help in this tempestuous country. The men had faith in his forecasts and it was decided that he should leave immediately for Attu on the United States Fishing Boat *Eider* so that he could send back reports. The *Eider* had a half-kilowatt spark transmitting set with a radius of 400 miles. Baker, the *Haida* radio officer, never ceased to wonder at the results the little ship achieved with her set. He thought the aerial was as unique as it was inefficient. It ran through stays and around masts and the insulation was leaky. For power there was only one set of storage batteries which were continually on charge when the ship was not transmitting.

The Chinese radio operator was sometimes relieved by the engineering officer when he was off duty.

The village of Nazan had a population of 79 Aleuts and one American school teacher. The fliers camped in a trading store and cooked their own food. One morning Smith, not exactly in the role of a commanding officer, cooked breakfast of ham and eggs and all the trimmings for the whole gang. It tasted good and they agreed that he was a pretty fair cook. The job of washing and drying dishes went to Arnold, Ogden and Harding. Another day, the native chief wanted a magneto fixed so a deal was made to repair it for two chickens which they boiled for dinner.

The radio set at Atka was worse than the *Eider's*. The Edison batteries had been exposed and the power plant had been used by one of the natives for a chicken coop. Water had damaged the receiver and the antenna had been used as a clothesline and rack for drying fish. Baker and the men of the *Haida* charged and cleaned the batteries, sent a spark coil ashore for use as a transmitter, fixed the receiver, cleaned the fish and clothes off the antenna and installed new insulation. Once again Atka was in touch with the outside world.

It was not, however, a favorite stopping off place. The five-foot beds, the rats, the limited food supply and the lethargic Aleuts did not excite them. The energetic fliers did not understand the Aleuts, who appeared uninterested in everything, especially work. Even the airplanes failed to fascinate them. They were practically speechless except to ask for four dollars an hour to guard the planes. The amount, outrageous for the time, almost left the fliers speechless. Tuberculosis was rampant among the natives and may have been one reason for their behavior. At best, Atka was a dreary place to live.

ALL REPORTS ABOUT Martin and Harvey were negative. The aviators kept telling each other that the two men were probably safe in some little harbor on the Bering Sea, but inwardly they knew that it was more likely that they had flown into a fog-covered peak. Day and night the search continued. At night searchlights swept the inlets, bays and small islands along the coast. One fear was that the *Seattle* had been blown out to sea by a northwest gale. An opposing opinion from a trapper sent others searching inland. Dogs crossed the portage from Chignik Lakes to the Bering Sea without success.

Seven days passed. The North American Newspaper Alliance offered $1000 as a reward to the person or persons who found Martin or Harvey, or who should give news of their whereabouts, dead or alive. The offer was broadcast to vessels in Alaskan waters, fishing canneries and trading posts in southwestern Alaska. The Coast Guard Cutter *Bear*, stationed at Seattle, prepared to carry a plane to Chignik to help search, but it would take two weeks. President Coolidge inquired daily at the War Department and issued a statement that every effort was being made to find "these gallant men."

Newspapers in the United States followed the flight, but only a major incident such as the disappearance of Martin and Harvey hit the front page, and then only briefly. More customary were a few lines on the back pages, if that much, from the Associated Press announcing the arrival or departure of the flight from one place to another with a rough flying time. Newspapermen could not sustain interest in the long, drawn-out event that seemed to be going nowhere. Mainly, it would have been a matter of printing delays and there was too much competing news to attract public interest. The Teapot Dome scandal monopolized headlines, the Republican and Democratic National Conventions were approaching and questions of war reparations and possible tax reductions ate up space.

ON THE OTHER side of the world, d'Oisy's smooth sailing had ceased. He had passed MacLaren as he sped to Agra, home of the Taj Mahal, but strong gusts of wind had badly shaken his plane. On landing he found that the heat had caused the fabric on the upper part of the plane to strip off. The damage was so bad he did not know if he could reach Calcutta. The heat had caused MacLaren trouble, too. While he was on the ground, he employed Indians to continually throw water on the hull to prevent cracking. The Portuguese fliers fared even worse. On May 8, they crashed at Pipar en route from Karachi to Agra. They planned to use a reserve plane, however, and were not finished.

WHEN SMITH, WADE and Nelson were leaving Chignik, an old sourdough named Osborne gave them a valuable tip. He told them that at a certain point a large valley would appear off to the right on a northerly heading. It would be inviting, but the wrong way to go. The correct track was straight ahead over a small pass. They followed his advice and it worked. Now, they felt certain that Martin had been deceived in bad weather by the wrong route.

MARTIN HAD TAKEN off at 11:00 A.M. The water and air were calm and the sky was overcast with clouds at about 500 feet. As they rounded Chignik Bay the air became turbulent and the plane bounced so much it took all of Martin's attention. Confused by mirages, and believing that he was off course, he swung south to the Pacific and crashed against a mountain shrouded in fog at an elevation of about 1500 feet above sea level. The plane had started slightly upward at the instant of impact on a slope, and that probably saved them.

Martin's first thought was for Harvey, but before he turned around he heard Harvey ask how he was. Miraculously, they were not hurt and jumped out of the plane and walked around the wreckage. When the realization of what had happened struck Martin he was overcome with utter despair. Hit with a deep depression, he felt that it would have been better to have perished in the crash. In a few minutes the mental agony passed and he joined Harvey who was quietly removing equipment from the baggage compartment. They selected necessities and prepared packs for their walk back to civilization. Then they sat down to eat a sandwich and have a cup of hot coffee. But there was no coffee. The thermos bottle had broken in the crash.

Plagued from the start, Martin now found that the emergency compass in his haversack did not work. Harvey came to the rescue with a small card compass in a leather case that a friend at Chanute Field had given to him the day he left, with the remark, "Take this, Al, you may find use for it some day."

Reluctantly, they took off their 11-pound flying suits and started walking in a white fog that blended so completely with the snow they really had to *watch* their step. About six inches of loose snow on top of an icy surface made walking difficult. Resting frequently and checking their position, they found that they were not walking in a straight course. Martin deviated to the left when he led, and Harvey deviated to the right. The two men wandered in the fog along the mountainside for three hours looking for a way down to the valley. They could not find a way and returned to the wreckage and built a fire out of the wings and broken pontoons. Chunks of ice made a windbreak against a northwesterly gale. They put on their flying suits again and crawled into the baggage compartment—a coffin-like space about seven feet long and about two and a half feet wide. The length was all right for the six-footers, but the width was a tight fit. It was at a 45 degree angle and Martin slept on the lower side. They fell asleep immediately but before long Martin felt that he was carrying the weight of a mountain. Harvey's 180 pounds had wedged him into a corner so that his right arm had become numb. In order to change position he had to wake Harvey and that ended sleep for the night. They thought the dawn would never come.

The next day the fog was so thick they remained with the plane. Their only food was concentrated liquids carried in two thermos bottles, so they limited themselves to two spoonfuls in water, three times a day. The mixture consisted of raisins, figs, walnuts, peanuts, barley, wheat and celery. It had the consistency of molasses and tasted as bitter and unpalatable as burnt sugar. One teaspoon supposedly constituted a meal.

The following day they set out and reached a valley and walked along a stream that they thought might take them to the ocean. It proved futile when they climbed a steep slope beyond. At the top of the mountain the fog lifted for a few minutes and to their horror they saw that they were four or five steps from walking off a cliff into a canyon about 1500 feet deep. There was no escape in that direction.

The mountains rose in a sheer wall of rock until they disappeared into the clouds. Lost in the wilderness, they camped in an alder thicket for the night. The fire of damp alder limbs failed to keep them warm and sleep was impossible.

Again they silently retraced their steps to the plane. After eight hours of climbing, Harvey was having trouble with his eyes and Martin thought he was becoming snowblind, too. At times it was almost a case of the blind leading the blind. Martin found some tablets of bichloride of mercury in one of the bags on the plane and made an eyewash for Harvey that restored his sight.

The next morning, still looking for a way out, they climbed the southeast side of the mountain till they were above the fog. From this vantage, they spotted a small lake for which they aimed the following day. They also saw some ptarmigan, a native bird of Alaska about the size of a ruffle grouse. Both Martin and Harvey were good shots, but the white birds made poor targets in the snow and they missed several times. Finally, they killed two. That night, the ptarmigan, added to their liquid rations, tasted like a rare delicacy. At last they had some solid food to chew and that was a psychological lift. The act of chewing made them feel like they were really eating something.

Martin's eyes were in such bad shape that Harvey led the way the next day, breaking trail. Occasionally Martin guided his course with a compass. He had not made a mistake in his choice of a flying companion, or a companion in adversity. He marveled at Harvey's dogged persistence as they broke through crusts of snow. Time and again they would plunge into the snow up to their waists and they would have to drag themselves out. It was exhausting work. They knew that they were becoming weaker and would have to find refuge soon. In the past few days their appearance had changed radically. Their faces were drawn and their cheeks sunken. They had not shaved or bathed, of course, and their hands, faces and even fingernails were a walnut color. The smoky fires caused some of the color. They also thought that the brown concentrated liquid rations might have permeated their systems until it stained their skin. That night they camped in a canyon near the lake and made beds of wild grass and alder bushes. For the first time they each slept about four hours at uneasy intervals.

Another night was spent in the canyon after a wasted day climbing another mountain. Each night they lost a little more strength, and collecting wood for the fire that night was an ordeal. While making camp they were too tired to bother about the nearby tracks of a Kodiak bear.

The morning of the seventh, after a night of severe cold, they heard the call of birds that sounded like wild geese. Then Harvey said, "Those birds are sea gulls." Martin knew that gulls seldom frequented fresh water and he said, "Thank God it's salt water." He was right. They were near the shore and could now use their hydrographic charts that were worthless inland. They did not know where they were but they were sure they could find out and celebrated with a smoke and conversation. Until then they had talked very little. Now they were exhilarated and jabbered away. Reaching the beach they were rid of the snow, and even better, they found a cabin when they rounded a point of land. No mansion ever looked so good. It was a trapper's cabin. Inside there was flour, canned milk and baking powder. They also found hardtack or dog biscuits. Whatever it was, they ate it. Looking further they came across salmon in brine, syrup, coffee, sugar and salt.

Martin read the directions on a can of baking power for flapjacks. It called for a quart of flour. Martin had his doubts that they could eat that much, but Harvey assured him that they could. While Martin started cooking, Harvey cleaned a grime-caked coffee pot. The hot cakes were a great success, but neither of them could eat more than two apiece. Their sense of taste was impaired—nothing tasted exactly right, and Harvey became deathly ill for a short time. They tossed for the canvas bed and Harvey won. Martin slept on a bin with a dirty mattress. The thought of pulling rank never entered his mind.

Exhausted, the men stayed in the cabin for three days. The second night a ferocious storm raged outside. They knew it had been a narrow escape. If they had not found the cabin they would have surely perished in the storm. Eventually the weather moderated and they felt stronger. One day Harvey rushed back from a reconnoitering trip with a report that there were two mallard ducks on the water about a hundred yards in front of the cabin. There was a 25:20 Winchester rifle in the cabin and Martin said, "Harvey, let me have that rifle, this is no time for amateurs." The water was shallow and the ducks were feeding on shell fish. Martin took careful aim and hit the male. The female took to the air and Martin, in a rush, missed the second shot. When the bird alighted about 200 yards away Martin showed off his prowess with a direct hit. Harvey was so pleased he acted like a schoolboy on vacation.

Soon, their luck began to change. While Harvey went on another expedition to check their whereabouts, Martin, feeling industrious and pleased with his triumph, swept out the cabin and found a portable oven in a gunnysack. Now he could roast the ducks. Then, about six o'clock in the evening, Harvey returned with two snowshoe rabbits that he had killed with the rifle. Not to be outdone, he proudly pointed out that he shot one while it was running. He also reported that he was sure they were on Moller Bay, about 25 miles from Port Moller. Reading a label on a case of canned milk in the cabin, they had learned that there was probably a cannery there.

Martin, filled with confidence as a cook, served the roasted duck for dinner. They were delighted. It was remarkable how well the two men, almost 20 years apart in age, had worked so well together. It was a tribute to both of them. Martin, however, almost lost his reputation as a cook by letting the biscuits burn and filling the room with smoke. Again Harvey was the perfect companion. It made no difference to him. He simply poured some syrup on the jet-black biscuits and declared that they were fine.

The next morning was the start of a big day. They fortified themselves with fried rabbit, hot cakes and cream gravy for breakfast, washed the dishes, put the cabin in order and left, ready to meet the world again. It was a beautiful day, and with their hopes up the hard hike seemed easy. About two o'clock in the afternoon they stopped to eat their lunch of roast duck, rabbit and hardtack and then took off again. Two hours later they spotted smoke from the cannery across the bay. The sight gave them a sense of security that they had not known for a long time. The world was a little closer. Swampy ground made the going rough. Taking a rest, Harvey noticed a launch coming their way. Five natives, two men and three women, were on their way to a hot spring when they noticed the strangers.

The natives recognized the aviators immediately since almost everyone in Alaska was looking for them. Taken to the cannery of the Pacific American Fisheries Company, they were given a royal welcome by the superintendent, a Mr. Amundson, and all the employees. No one could have asked for better treatment—delicious food, baths and clean beds. Radiograms went out to the other fliers, to Patrick and, most important, to their families. As pleased as Martin and Harvey were to be back in civilization they also knew that their flight had ended on that bleak mountainside.

This is what Martin and Harvey looked like when they came in from the cold of their Alaskan ordeal.

Martin's radio message arrived in Washington, D.C. on May 11. It was sent from Port Moller to Dutch Harbor to Pearl Harbor, Hawaii, to the Navy Department. Addressed to the Chief of Air Service it gave the brief details of their survival and credit to the concentrated food that kept them alive during their darkest days. It ended, "Awaiting instructions here." Patrick replied:

WE REJOICE AND THANK GOD THAT YOU ARE BOTH SAFE AND WELL. CONFIDENCE IN YOU UNABATED. YOU HAVE PROVED YOURSELF. STILL WANT YOU TO COMMAND FLIGHT. CANNOT ARRANGE FOR YOU TO OVERTAKE OTHERS BY GOING WEST. YOU AND SERGEANT HARVEY WILL REPORT TO ME HERE WITHOUT DELAY. PLAN TO SEND YOU EAST TO REJOIN FLIGHT AT FURTHEST CONVENIENT POINT FROM WHICH YOU CAN COMPLETE THE JOURNEY WITH THE REST OF YOUR COMMAND.

In San Diego, Martin's wife, in anguish, expected to learn the worst until a messenger boy appeared at the door with a big smile. She knew he had good news. The message said:

HELLO DEAREST. SAFE AT PORT MOLLER, 6PM TODAY. CRASHED AGAINST MOUNTAIN IN FOG 30TH. NEITHER HURT. SURVIVED NEXT TEN DAYS. GOOD HEALTH. DRY YOUR TEARS. FRED.

The news did not seem so wonderful to Martin's little boy who did not know that his father was missing. He burst into tears when he learned that his father was out of the world flight. The jubilant Mrs. Martin said that she was going to ask her husband to promise never to fly again. It would be a promise never made.

Befitting the occasion, the mothers of Martin and Harvey received the good news on Mother's Day.

A fisheries steamer, the *Catherine D*, returned the two fliers to the state of Washington. During the voyage Harvey was guest of honor at a party celebrating his 24th birthday. The party was Martin's idea. He knew how to keep a stiff upper lip. When they reached Bellingham, Washington, a band and about a thousand people greeted them to help soften the disappointment.

In the meantime, radio communications from Blair on the *Eider* at Attu were poor and it was difficult to receive weather reports early enough in the day to be useful for the flight from Atka. Serious thought was given to bringing the *Eider* back part way to Kiska so that the base for the British flight could be used. Their British rivals were more co-operative than competitive; they had offered the Americans the use of any of their advance bases. On May 9, however, a satisfactory weather report arrived from Blair and the planes left for Attu, a rugged island that rose more than 4000 feet in the air.

Shortly after the *New Orleans* left the water, Nelson almost crashed. Making a turn he ran into a "woolie," a strong down current of air, that blew him back onto the water while traveling at about 85 miles per hour. The others watched helplessly, sure that only his skill could save the plane. Nelson gave credit to the pontoons that withstood the impact without damage. Fighting strong winds, the long, cold flight over water arrived at Attu, a distance of 555 miles, after eight hours and fifty-five minutes. Their progress had been slow, but now they were at the western tip of the desolate Aleutian Islands, the jumping-off place for Japan. Could they beat the rough North Pacific? All they could do was plan carefully and hope for the best.

About 6:30 A.M., on the morning of the eleventh, Harding, more asleep than awake, thought he heard two of the crew on the *Eider* talking in a low tone about the Major being found the night before. Was he dreaming? He jumped out of the little bunk and asked what they had said. It was not a dream. The *Haida* had picked up the good news about 11:00 P.M. the night before on the way to Attu. Harding had a definite feeling of relief. A heavy burden on all of their minds lifted. The men on the *Eider* shouted for joy and everyone felt much better. Death had not touched the world flight.

Smith was now acting commander and it was a heavy responsibility for the young lieutenant. A First Lieutenant commanding two other skillful First Lieutenants with their own ideas about flying was not an enviable task and may even have been a little awkward. Always re-served, Smith possibly became a little more so. He was not an easy man to know, but his reserve could never be mistaken for lack of confidence. He was a self-assured person who knew his business and was respected by everyone. A sergeant under him once paid the highest compliment any commander can receive by describing him as "tough but fair." After a strenuous month they were moving into unknown waters and there were many difficult decisions ahead. Judgment was and is an important part of flying. When to fly or not to fly was always critical, and patience was not an easy virtue in the battle against anxiety. One error in judgment could mean the end. Smith, consulting with Wade and Nelson, made the final decisions. At Attu they waited again.

MEANWHILE, THE UNITED States Navy, under orders from Secretary of the Navy Denby, gave full cooperation to the Air Service. The high level service jealousies that swirled around Washington were of no concern to the commanders of the American destroyers *Ford* and *Pope*. They carried fuel and spare parts for the world flight and had waited in the wretched Kuriles since mid-April. Nutt remained in Tokyo near the center of activity because there were still misgivings about the Japanese. In his place he detailed an American language officer to accompany each destroyer with specific instructions. Although relations with the Japanese improved, the captain of the *Pope*, Lt. Commander John McClaren, found some of their transparent lies irritating and he protested. After his protest, the Japanese reversed themselves, but McClaren thought that their behavior was "engendered by [an] inferiority complex characteristic of Japanese officialdom."

On the way north, skirting ice floes in rough weather, the ships investigated Bettobu Bay, one of the approved landing areas. It was nothing more than an open roadstead and quite unsatisfactory. Another bay near the center of the southeast coast of Yetorofu looked better, but neither Lt. Saburo Yamaguchi, a naval aviator, nor Captain Masao Yamase of the Army General Staff, the two liason officers on the *Ford*, could grant permission to land there. However, when they finally sent a message to Tokyo, approval arrived the following day.

At Yetorofu, three Japanese destroyers, the *Tokitsukaze, Isokaze* and *Amatsukaze*, joined the Americans to watch their movements. They knew the dangers of these waters at this time of year, but they had no intention of giving these strange foreigners a completely free hand.

The *Ford*, accompanied by two of the Japanese destroyers, sailed northward to Kashiwabara Bay, Paramushiru, and stood vigil in extremely disagreeable weather, rolling 15 degrees one way, and then 15 degrees the other way. The barometer fluctuated widely and tide rips threatened to pile the destroyer on the rocks. One day, caught in a whirlpool, the ship swung broadside to the current and started dragging toward the nearby destroyer *Tokitsukaze*. A second anchor, dropped in a minute, held the ship. If it had not, the collision could have brought about a nasty international incident.

Fifty years earlier the volcanic islands had been a hunting ground for sea otter. Now they and about 170 different species of birds were almost extinct. At Yetorofu there was a small colony of Japanese and Ainu fishermen, but at Paramushiru, located at the northern end of the Kurile chain, the only inhabitants were two Japanese who worked for a cannery and had been isolated there for 18 months. The two men mistook a landing party for Russian pirates and hid until they learned that their visitors meant them no harm. When Ensign McCullom, the language officer on the *Ford*, explained that they were Americans they received an invitation to lunch.

Linton Wells, the Associated Press correspondent on board the *Ford*, published a six page, foolscap size newspaper that he called the Paramushiru *Breeze*. After a few days, everyone agreed to change the name to the Paramushiru *Gale*. Through the newspaper the sailors learned that Martin had been forced down and later lost. Now they had no idea when the flight would arrive.

While waiting at sea, the Japanese officers on the *Tokitsukaze* invited the Americans aboard and professed their good will. In a spirit of cordiality, several of their enlisted men sang national songs and then a Japanese officer sang *The Star Spangled Banner* in English. Ensign McCollum, equal to the occasion, answered by singing their national anthem in Japanese. When the Americans left the ship they received an enthusiastic sendoff with many "banzais" and much waving of hats.

Two nights later, Lt. Commander Holloway Frost, captain of the *Ford*, invited the Japanese officers to a buffet dinner and motion pictures in the wardroom. Commander Morita, commander of the Eighteenth Destroyer Flotilla, made a polite speech saying how glad he was that the Japanese Navy was able to assist the flight. He claimed that it was a small return for friendship dating back to Commodore Matthew Perry, who had introduced Japan to the ways of the western world. Lt. Commander Wada, captain of the *Tokitsukaze*, said he noticed how well the enlisted men of both nations helped each other, which was quite true. Less than 18 years later, the four stacker *Ford*, along with the *Pope,* would meet the Japanese Navy in the Macassar Straits under unfriendlier circumstances. Men on the *Ford* would boast that they were the first American ship to sink an enemy ship by gunfire since Manila Bay.

THERE WAS UNDOUBTEDLY an element of sincerity in their present expressions of goodwill, forced or not. Curiosity, if nothing else, created an intriguing interest on both sides that made their evenings together enjoyable. As sailors they also shared the dangers of this vile area. It was an experience that formed a special comradeship. Still, this was not a happy time in Japanese-American relations. At this very moment the United States Congress, responding to agitation in California, was considering an immigration bill that would exclude Japanese. As recently as 1923, the Supreme Court of the United States ruled that Japanese, being neither free white persons nor persons of African nativity and descent, might not be naturalized under existing statutes. President Coolidge opposed the new immigration bill before Congress that contained a clause declaring all aliens ineligible for citizenship as an affront to the Japanese. Nevertheless, on May 26, 1924, the bill would become the Johnson Immigration Act. Coolidge, in a political corner, did not use his veto.

Bitterness in the United States increased to such a pitch that the *Literary Digest* commented at the time that some newspapers placed the Japanese so low on the racial scale as to prompt the question: "Are Japanese people?" Expressions of goodwill were not as evident in Washington or Tokyo as they were in Paramushiru. The Japanese Ambassador to the United States sent a note of protest to the Secretary of State and the *Tokyo Kokumin* observed that the exclusion bill illustrated a definite expression of anti-Japanism and "makes the situation graver than ever before."

The Japanese must have been confused by the American attitude. The previous September a great earthquake had destroyed a third of Tokyo as well as most of Yokohama and had killed more than 140,000 people. No nation had helped the stricken country more than the United States. Even more confusing, while the exclusion bill moved through Congress, the United States floated a $150 million loan to

Japan, the largest international loan since World War I, to help repair earthquake damage. The *New York Herald* reported that there was no opposition to the loan in any of the western states that were supposed to hold such anti-Japanese sentiments.

MEANWHILE, THE MEN on the *Ford* and *Tokitsukaze* simply coped with the sea. The *Ford* and *Pope* set up radio communications with the *Eider* via the Coast Guard Cutter *Haida*, but little word arrived about the fliers. Communications were erratic and the radio stations at the bases at Ominato and Soya never answered messages from the destroyers. All they could do was wait.

For the time being, the *Ford* had relatively good weather. The men of the *Pope*, on station to the south, were not so lucky. The captain of the *Pope* used every ounce of seamanship battling winds varying from force ten to force twelve for over twelve hours. On the Beaufort scale, force twelve is a hurricane with winds over 73 miles per hour and "phenomenal" waves over 55 feet. It was a horrifying experience, but the *Pope* survived.

On April 30, His Majesty's Canadian Ship *Thiepval*, a 125-foot, coal-burning steam trawler, normally used for tending lighthouses, anchored near the *Ford*. Colonel Broome of the Royal Air Service Reserve, the advance officer for the British world flight, had set out from Vancouver on March 1 to collect and substantiate information. He visited the *Ford* and exchanged data with Commander Frost while the wind blew a near gale for several hours. Broome, a friendly man, had his own adventurous cruise while scouting the Aleutians, Komandorski Islands and Kamchatka. Unlike the Americans, the British had friendlier diplomatic relations with the Russians and they permitted him ashore. Although his resources were not the match of the American's, he offered the use of his buoys to Frost and later sent valuable information to the *Ford* by dispatch. When Broome approached Hakodate, Japan, a few days later, he wrote in his diary:

Strong gale ahead of course . . . how this little ship stands the pounding is more than I can tell. She is now light as a cork . . . all coal burnt . . . all cargo out . . . stores consumed . . . so she rears out of water half her length and is pounded on the bottom by the next wave like blows of a giant sledge hammer . . . We are red with rust . . . stern grating smashed . . . filthy dirty, but—THE JOB IS DONE . . . have come through six thousand miles of North Pacific in March, April, and May . . head gales always except around the Komandorskis and Kamchatka and have been the first boat of the year in all the harbours we made.

The men on the *Ford* and *Pope* could appreciate Broome's accomplishments.

Days went by and the *Ford* ran short of food and fuel and the men went on reduced rations. On May 3, the *Pope* came alongside as strong winds increased to force seven and transferred fuel and all the stores that could be spared so that the *Ford* could make a 900 mile run to Hakodate where she would be resupplied by the USS *Perry* and *Truxton*. The *Pope* remained at Paramushiru.

On the return trip to Paramushiru the *Ford* rode through an easterly gale that worked up to force eight with waves 30 to 40 feet high. The visibility was very low and the oscillator soundings showed the ship in close proximity to land. Despite the possibility of impending disaster, the ship's position could not be fixed for 48 hours. The barometric pressure dropped to 28.65 inches. The ship rolled 35 degrees a side at times and once rolled 53 degrees to starboard in the massive waves. It seemed as though she would never right herself again. Yet she did and rode well through the rough sea. Frost was pleased to see that the *Ford* seldom took on water, even when plowing through the huge waves.

AT ATTU, THE fliers lived aboard the crowded *Eider* where they were well cared for by Captain Johannssen Beck, an old hand in these northern waters. They knew that Beck was a good man to have with them in tough times and would never forget his resourcefulness. He must have been an unusual man to have impressed the aviators so much. And the crew was as congenial as it was tough. The small diesel engine boat was especially valuable because it could enter Aleutian harbors where the shallowness of water prevented larger vessels from entering.

A few hours after their arrival at Attu a severe storm started that kept them grounded for several days. So far, the flight had been nothing but a series of delays. Held up four days in Prince Rupert, three days in Sitka, two days in Seward, three days at Chignik and 14 days at Dutch Harbor, they were losing the battle against time. Now they waited again.

During the delay they checked and rechecked their charts with bad weather on their minds. It was decided to head northwest in the direction of Cape Kronatski on the Russian Kamchatka Peninsula so that their course would be within sight of land the greater part of the flight. Then they would fly south from that point along the Kamchatka coast to Paramushiru. The *Eider*, with Bissell on board, parted company with the fliers and took up station off the Komandorski Islands where they sent weather reports back to the Coast Guard Cutter *Haida* which, in turn, relayed them to the shore station at Attu. The men on the *Haida* had taken ashore a Signal Corps receiver and a transmitting set that they had built on the ship while sailing north. It consisted of four five-watt tubes in parallel and enough battery power for 48 hours of continuous operation. The range for sending and receiving messages was 200 miles.

Wells, the newspaperman on the *Ford*, hoping for his big story to arrive any day, had temporarily transferred to the *Pope* when the *Ford* made its run for food and fuel. Instead of a front page story he had a harrowing time that hardly made the papers. Later, he wrote,

Picture the scene: Three destroyers—two Japanese, one American—are anchored in a shallow bight off a narrows which flows between the adjacent headlands into an ocean of mountainous waves. The wind strikes at these vessels with a velocity of more than 100 miles an hour and shrieks with fury when it fails to destroy them. Their anchors drag . . . To put to sea would probably mean disaster, so their skippers attempt to keep them where they are. By the night of May 9 the storm was so violent it was like a bad dream. Captain McClaren would allow the wind to push the *Pope*, time and again, as far across the bay as he thought it safe to go, then maneuver into the wind, put on speed, and regain his position. "Crawfishing" he explained.

The storm continued for three days and everyone gave up hope of ever seeing the world flight. One evening as conditions grew worse, McClaren, weary from battling the sea, stopped briefly in the wardroom and told Wells and Major Bratten, the Army language officer, to put on life preservers. He knew it was an idle gesture because they could not last a minute in the icy water. They wondered how the ship could pull through. But it did pull through. When, a few months later, McClaren's hair turned gray, Wells was sure that it had been caused by those desperate days and nights.

On May 12, the *Ford* reappeared to relieve the *Pope*, which had actually passed through two violent gales while standing by at Kashiwabara. A Japanese merchant vessel of 1000 tons was lost with eight men aboard only three miles from the *Pope's* anchorage. Frost wrote in his official report that only the skill and courage of Lt. Commander McClaren had saved the ship.

THE WEATHER IMPROVED in the Kuriles and the *Ford*, back on station at Paramushiru, sent a despatch to the *Haida* recommending that the planes start immediately, only to receive a reply that the weather was unfavorable at Attu. On May 13, the bottom dropped out of the barometer there and fell below 28.60 inches. On May 15, a strong force-nine gale still lingered there. It seemed as though decent weather would never prevail in both places at the same time. The realization dawned on the fliers that they were up against worse odds than expected. The big question was how to cross this unpredictable stretch of water and stay alive. What was the best route? When should they risk a takeoff? Conditions would probably never be *perfect*.

Searching for a solution to their problems, they decided that the Russian coastline looked more inviting since they carried neither a radio nor direction finder. Pilots, not diplomats, were laying their lives on the line. Smith sent a despatch to the *Ford* on the 13th that showed the extent of their desperation. He asked that a destroyer investigate landing places along the Kamchatka coast. Frost was certain that such movements would arouse suspicions and create diplomatic difficulties and gave the only reply possible. He answered that it could not be done without an entire change of plans, a long delay and the permission of the State Department.

On the 16th, the weather was good at Paramushiru and the *Ford* continued to forward regular weather reports. Still, there was no word from the fliers. During the forenoon of the 17th the winds increased and the weather grew worse.

V

NORTH TO THE ORIENT

ON MAY 15, the weather looked good at both ends and the pilots decided it was now or never. The three planes left on the first flight ever for Japan at 11:25 A.M. They continued on their way, north, or more precisely northwest, to the Orient. The *Haida*, a true guardian angel, sailed ahead on a straight line to the northwest so that the aircraft could fly over the ship to check their compasses. As Attu faded away the last link with America also faded away. What perils lay ahead? All they could see before them were thick clouds and rain squalls.

Flying through impenetrable fog, snow and rain, and buffeted by winds that threatened to rip off the fabric of the planes, the compass was their sole guide across the Pacific. There was no time for doubt or fear, but certainly each man had his own inner thoughts as they moved into the unknown. To say that they were fearless would be foolish. They were not insensitive to the hazards of the North Pacific. The past few weeks of relentless winds and faulty engines had taught them terrifying lessons. With one plane down and three to go, would this be like the case of the ten little Indians?

Their flying instruments were few: a tachometer, an electric meter, an oil pressure gauge, a gas gauge and an altimeter. The pilots occasionally dropped a smoke bomb to figure drift and wind direction by sighting along a peg placed on the centerline of the fuselage at the rear of the aft cockpit. Lines painted down over the empennage and across the stabilizer fanned out in five degree increments. They sighted down the lines to determine drift and corrected their course accordingly. When they found that a strong north wind blew, they crabbed a little to compensate. There were also turn and bank indicators. The turn indicator operated by a small wind-driven cog which worked a pointer that allowed the pilot to put the plane back on course. The banking indicator operated on an inertia basis. Whenever the plane turned gently, or with the proper amount of speed, the pointer remained at zero.

About an hour out of Attu the planes arrived over the *Haida*, circled

These are the few simple tools that the fliers had to help them find their way around the world.

in bombing formation, and crossed again to check their course with the ship. Planks painted black laid out on the deck in prearranged order signaled the weather ahead. Then the planes disappeared over the horizon. They had a deep affection for the captain and crew of the *Haida* who had always been so anxious to help. Leaving them behind was painful.

Flying over the sea was a lonely and dangerous business. Harding wrote in his diary, "If one were to concede to their thoughts they would turn back but being three in number is a wonderful consolation. T'would be out of the ordinary for 3 such planes and engines to fail at the same time."

Time passed slowly with only the sky above, the water below and trouble looming ahead. At 1:15 P.M. they hit a snowstorm. Suddenly, everything was a uniform gray color and it was impossible to see. To avoid the snow they headed north instead of west and finally gave up hope of reaching Paramushiru that day. They decided to head for the Komandorski Islands in forbidden Russian territory. On they went and later in the afternoon sighted land ahead. "No wonder Columbus got a thrill," Harding wrote. Three hours over open sea and Smith hit the mark. It was a masterpiece of navigation. The time was 4:50 P.M. and the date May 14, since they had crossed the International Date Line and lost 24 hours. The *Eider* "happened" to be standing by so when the planes showed up, the little boat ran close to shore, dropped buoys and the planes landed.

The *Haida*, continuing westward behind the planes, had received a message from the *Eider* that the planes had "dropped into Nicholski" in the Komandorskis and she headed for a position off the island. In the latter part of April, Captain Hottel of the *Haida* had received confidential orders from the commander of the Bering Sea Patrol Force. He anticipated possible difficulties for the flight and gave Hottel authority to convoy the planes across the Pacific until contact was made with the Destroyer Force of the United States Navy's Asiatic Fleet. If considered expedient in the captain's judgment, the cutter could safeguard the planes to the Kurile Islands and call at Hakodate for fuel and fresh water.

The orders also covered a possible forced landing on the Russian coast or at one of their islands. In that event the orders read, "You are authorized, under emergency procedure, to proceed within the territorial waters of Russia, for the purpose of rendering assistance to, or

rescuing the planes and personnel in distress, but will not effect a landing on shore with the cutter's boats or crew, nor engage in any commercial transactions with the Subjects of Russia, unless circumstances
are *most urgent* and clearly demand such action in the cause of hu-
manity." When the Coast Guard agreed to cooperate, they meant
what they said, and their cooperation was at considerable risk, poli-
tically and personally.

The surprised Russians called on their unexpected visitors aboard
the *Eider* to find out what they were doing there and who gave them
authority for entering the area. Through Captain Beck and a crew
member who understood some Russian, they explained their plight.
Despite their calm demeanors, the Americans knew that they had no
business being there. The courteous Russians did not show the least
sign of hostility and sent a radio message to the Soviet government re-
questing permission for the party to come ashore. In that part of the
world visitors were a rare treat, but their impersonal government
thought otherwise. In the morning word came from Moscow that the
Americans would have to leave immediately. Meanwhile the storm had
been ridden out for six dark hours and they were ready to go. At five in
the morning it was light enough to work. Prop covers came off, engines
uncovered and sea anchors pulled in. Wade thought he saw men holding rifles in a boat. He did not wait to check his impression. They took
off in long, smooth swells without any trouble.

Onward they continued. For a while the weather was ideal and soon
after, flying due west, they could clearly see the snow-covered mountains of Kamchatka. The last half of the flight was different. They flew
over fog, under fog and through snowstorms down the coast to Paramushiru. Often they were unable to fly over the fog because their
maximum altitude with pontoons was only 7000 feet. Finally they
reached their destination in a rain and windstorm. The distance was
585 miles; the flying time was six hours and forty-five minutes. Since
Attu they had flown almost 1000 miles and amazed themselves with
the accuracy of their navigation. When Paramushiru came into view
they were only about a mile off in their calculations.

The planes circled the *Ford* several times and from the air they
could see both Japanese and American crews waving on deck. A signalman on watch on the four stack destroyer was the first to sight the
planes. Up to that time the *Ford* had no word that the aircraft had
left Attu. Fortunately all gear was ready for their reception. In this

forlorn spot all service and national jealousies vanished with the thrill
of the three planes appearing out of nowhere. The *Ford* sounded its
siren for the first men to cross the Pacific by air and the two Japanese
destroyers joined the ovation. Smith made fast to a buoy laid by Broome
and the others secured their planes to buoys laid by the *Ford*.

A minute or two before their arrival, Linton Wells, back on the
Ford, had gone to the wireless shack and placed his daily message.
He was having a tough time keeping a dead story alive. Like most of his
previous reports, he described the foul weather and put off the estimated time for the flight to show up. Then he walked out on deck
where wet snow was falling and glanced over the bow toward the en-
trance to Little Kurile Strait. For a few seconds he scarcely realized
what he saw: three planes in triangle formation. He rushed back to the
radio room, killed his previous message and scribbled a few words that
the planes had arrived. Then he ran to his cabin for his camera and
went on deck again. This time he could see Smith and Wade waving
as they circled. A little later he gave the radio operator several hundred
words and finally scored a world news beat.

A major step had been taken in reaching their goal, but the aviators
had little time for self-congratulations. Since morning the weather had
grown worse. The wind had increased and shifted to the east with
heavy snow falling. Moored in an unprotected channel between Paramushiru and Shimushu Island, the *Boston* and *New Orleans* were
open to strong currents, tide rips and winds. During the night the
storm intensified to a gale and the planes pitched so badly in ten-foot
waves they almost turned turtle. The winds had a clear sweep of about
a mile before reaching the planes. The *Ford* rolled as much as 24
degrees a side. Nelson thought it was one of the most frightening experiences of the trip. The destruction of the planes seemed almost a
certainty. It was impossible to board them in the rough sea and everyone feared they would be lost. All the men could do was worry. No one
slept much that night on the rolling ship and the next afternoon when
the winds fell and clouds lifted, they were surprised to find the planes
were still there. One reason that they survived probably was that the
elevators were tied in a diving position. The harder it blew, the more
the planes would squat down. The *Ford* sent out a boat so that the
moorings could be examined. They found the quarter-inch bridles that
held the planes were badly worn and one plane had only one un-
broken strand left out of seven.

Only three planes made it to the *Ford*, but at least now they knew
that Martin and Harvey were alive.

When the *Haida* learned that the planes had left the Komandorskis, she rendezvoused with the *Eider* and took Lieutenant Bissell aboard. Still, the *Haida* proceeded along the line of flight. Later, when the cutter received a message that the planes had landed in the Kuriles, the captain changed course 180 degrees but slowed down to await word as to whether or not she was needed further. By evening no word ar-arrived and she headed for Dutch Harbor, to the great disappointment of all hands.

Some hours later a message arrived that the cutter could not land in the Kuriles without permission from the Imperial Japanese Government. Smith reported that the *Haida* would be good insurance, but there was no immediate need for her services. If there had been an emergency there is little doubt that the *Haida* would have shown up whether or not anyone gave her permission.

One man on the *Haida* must have sighed with relief as he sailed towards Dutch Harbor. He was Clayton Bissell. Aside from mopping up, his task was over. He had handled a thousand details, plus the extra duty of searching for Martin and Harvey. It was a high-pressure job that he'd done well. He must have found some satisfaction in the Air Service because he held a law degree and could have swapped the frenzy for a quiet law practice in his hometown of Kane, Pennsylvania, anytime, but he never did.

When things calmed down, the fliers read many messages of congratulations. One, to "Members of the World Flight" from Secretary of War Weeks read:

CONGRATULATIONS PERIOD YOURS IS THE HONOR OF BEING THE FIRST TO CROSS THE PACIFIC BY AIR PERIOD THROUGH ITS ARMY AND NAVY OUR COUNTRY HAS THE HONOR OF HAVING LED IN THE CROSSING OF BOTH GREAT OCEANS PERIOD THE ARMY HAS EVERY FAITH IN YOUR ABILITY TO ADD THE CIRCUMNAVIGATION OF THE GLOBE TO ITS ACHIEVEMENTS.

It picked up their spirits. The journey had been far more difficult than they had anticipated and they appreciated the boost. Since Seattle they had been out of touch with civilization and it was good to hear from home.

The commander of one of the Japanese destroyers invited the fliers aboard for a light lunch while waiting for the storm to clear. He served brandy, Sauterne, red wine, Scotch and sake, hot and cold. Arnold claimed that no one got tipsy during the pleasant afternoon, but if the Japanese had an ulterior motive and hoped to loosen the tongues of their guests they were wasting their time. The Americans had a far better capacity than their hosts.

Eventually the weather improved and the flight worked its way down the Kuriles to Hitokappu, Yetorofu Island, where the *Pope* waited. It was here, 17 years later, that the Japanese task force rendezvoused for their attack on Pearl Harbor. The fog was so thick the day the fliers arrived that the launch sent to pick them up had to steer by compass.

On May 22, everyone had breakfast at midnight and prepared for an early takeoff. Before the day was over they spent nine and a half hours in the air. Their first stop was Minato, a fishing village on the northeast coast of Honshu. Cliff Nutt greeted them and he was ready with the supplies they needed. He had sampans with gasoline, oil and water, and an interpreter on each one to handle the language problem. They refueled and repaired a short circuit in the battery on the *Chicago*, but did not go ashore, to the disappointment of school children from the surrounding hillsides who waved American flags and sang American patriotic songs they had just learned. The fliers were probably more disappointed than the children as they looked towards the picturesque village tucked away in a valley. The grass was green, trees were in bloom and, above all, there was no snow.

In the afternoon, the flight reached Kasumigaura Naval Air Station, 50 miles north of Tokyo. Farmers, hip deep in flooded rice paddies, dropped their mattocks and rushed to the shore to see the sight. The pilots had flown 835 miles, the longest day's journey up to then, and had closed the last gap in man's aerial navigation around the world. The Americans, British and Portuguese had flown across the Atlantic, the British had flown from England to Singapore and the Italians had crossed southern Asia and moved up the China coast. Since Seattle, the Army fliers had flown 5657 miles in 76 hours and 18 minutes in the air. American flags, "banzais" and fireworks filled the air. Any bitterness over the exclusion question was either forgotten or submerged for the time being. Among the thousands who witnessed the landing were the Commander of the Japanese Imperial Navy, the Minister of War and Commanders of the Japanese Army and Navy Air Services. Twenty leading residents of nearby Tsuchiura wore stars and stripes badges on their best silk kimonos. The immaculate Japanese made a sharp contrast with the Americans in their oil-stained flying suits and un-shaven, weatherbeaten faces. They looked healthy and competent, but hardly neat or imposing. At a reception in a hangar, a table was spread with chestnuts signifying triumph and dried fish for good luck, both old warrior emblems.

Major General Yasumitsu said to the fliers, "You have already gained a name comparable to Perry." Commordore Perry's name would come up often in the next few days. Yasumitsu, wearing a new smile, was the same man who had blocked Cliff Nutt at every turn. The about-face in behavior was carried off without the slightest embarrass-ment. Nutt must have muttered to himself as he observed the complete change in attitude. Smith replied for the group by saying that it was a great pleasure to emerge from the raw north into the balminess of Japan.

The next evening 40 geisha girls performed a special dance in their honor at a banquet given by the commander of the Tsuchiura naval base. After taking off their shoes, the fliers sat down on straw matting in a large room and had tea with a number of English-speaking Army and Navy officers. After a half hour of polite conversation they went into the banquet room. Each girl, dressed in colorful silks, cared for a single guest at a separate low table. To Arnold, who always enjoyed a good time, it seemed like a dream.

The social schedule was cut to a minimum, but there were recep-tions, banquets and fetes wherever they went. Two days were spent in Tokyo where huge crowds welcomed them. It was estimated that there were 10,000 people at the railroad station when they arrived. From there they were driven in a Hudson and a Cadillac to the Imperial Hotel. Designed by the American architect Frank Lloyd Wright, the hotel had withstood last year's shattering earthquake while much of the city was wiped out. Wright had become one of the best known Americans in Japan.

Smith insisted upon equal honors for all of the men and emphasized that the mechanics were as important as the pilots. As leader of the flight, Smith could have easily accepted all of the honors for himself. It was not an uncommon practice for flight commanders to monopo-lize the glory. By a curious coincidence, the Japanese were more than ready to make Smith their special hero. In 1916, Art Smith, known widely as the "boy aviator," had stirred up wild enthusiasm in Japan by

Lt. Smith became the flight leader once it became clear that Martin couldn't catch up with them.

looping the loop and performing other reckless acrobatics in a high wind. It was Japan's first real introduction to aviation. Patrick said at the time that the greatest flying feats ever seen by Japanese were accomplished by men named Smith and the impression was implanted in their minds that all Americans with that name must be wonderful aviators. Another Smith, Herbert Smith, an Englishman, probably impressed the Japanese militarists even more. He had designed combat aircraft for Sopwith during World War I and had gone to Japan in 1921 to study the needs of the Imperial Navy. The Japanese wanted a fighter plane to be used on the *Hosho*, their first aircraft carrier, and Smith designed a plane for them that became the Mitsubishi 1MF1. Despite the preeminence of air-minded Smiths in Japan, Lowell Smith turned down any special attention for himself. No one had less interest in personal publicity. He also backed up his words with one other gesture. He requested Ogden's promotion to Second Lieutenant.

In Tokyo they met General Nagoaka, the President of the Japanese Aviation Society, and had lunch with General Ugaki, the Minister of War, in a friendly atmosphere. They were also the honored guests at a lunch given by the faculty of the University of Tokyo. Members of the Aeronautical Research Institute of Japan were present too. The fliers thoroughly enjoyed themselves and saw no signs of belligerence. One correspondent, perhaps in an attempt to create copy, thought that there was less enthusiasm when the aviators appeared in uniform instead of their flying clothes.

WHILE THE JAPANESE did their best to be good hosts, President Coolidge signed the Immigration Bill. Secretary of State Hughes had previously argued that the exclusion provision was quite unnecessary and the President said if that section had stood alone he would have disapproved it without hesitation. Nevertheless, his hand was forced because the Quota Act of 1921 would soon terminate, and the new bill included much-needed administrative machinery. Despite their misgivings, Senator Henry Cabot Lodge considered the bill the most important measure passed by Congress in his 30 years in that body. The author of the Senate bill, Reed of Pennsylvania, believed that its adoption would mean that the "America of our grandchildren will be a vastly better place to live in. It will mean a more homogeneous nation, more self reliant, more independent, and more closely knit by common purpose and common ideas." The *Cincinnati Enquirer* agreed. The newspaper boldly stated, "The crux of this matter is that the United States, like Canada and Australia, must be kept a white man's country."

These actions did not go unnoticed in Japan. The *Osaka Mainichi* held that the decision of Congress was an "insult to Japan and the Japanese," and the *Tokyo Nichi Nichi* wrote, "Disturbers of the peace are the anti-Japanese members of the American Congress, while we are advocates of peace." In the next few weeks some Japanese would commit harakiri as a protest against the new law.

A correspondent for the *Chicago Tribune* reported that four imperial princesses of Japan visited the airfield where the World Cruisers were located without meeting the pilots or viewing the machines. The Prince Regent, later Emperor Hirohito, did not receive the American airmen, contrary to announcements that he would. Some Tokyo stores displayed signs, "No American Goods Sold Here" in a move to boycott American merchandise. The Japanese jingoist press did their best to intensify anti-American sentiments. A cartoon in the *Tokyo Miyako*, shortly after the airmen's visit, showed Uncle Sam as two-faced, but none of these attitudes were evident to the world fliers.

In the United States, the *Pittsburgh Sun* commented that the Japanese, with their sensibilities wounded by the exclusion measure, might have been rather cold to the fliers. "Instead their message of congratulations shows genuine admiration and sincere good-will in every phase." The *St. Louis Globe-Democrat* idealistically wrote, "Now that their islands have been brought within flying radius (they) may wonder what, from their standpoint, it may all mean in peace and what it all may mean in war. But while it is easier to induce apprehension than a feeling of security, is not the great lesson of the flight rather a lesson of peace?"

WHILE EACH NATION had trouble seeing the other clearly, the aviators found themselves the target of autograph seekers, reporters and photographers. Smith always spoke reluctantly and modestly, but one thing bothered him. Everyone referred to them as "Magellans of the Air." He said that as he remembered, quite correctly, Magellan met his death in his attempt to circle the world shortly after crossing the Pacific. Smith did not plan to follow in his footsteps.

Within earshot of reporters, the frank Nelson made a slighting remark about the slow moving Aleuts. He thought they were the laziest people in the world and said so. "They wanted four dollars an hour to help us. We paid two dollars which was two dollars more than it was worth." The press in the United States picked up the remark and before long Smith received a reminder from Washington for the crews to be cautious about statements to newspapermen. They were celebrities now as well as representatives of the United States and had to watch their words.

While dressing in their rooms at the Imperial Hotel for a reception, Colonel Broome, the advance officer for the British world flight, showed up. He found a merry, tousle-headed group running in and out in various stages of dress. As he watched them, it occurred to him that he was twice the age of the Americans and had a son older than the youngest flier. But age did not affect their friendship. There was too much to talk about. While happily chatting about their common experiences, there was a knock on the door. Someone had a message for Broome. He read it without a word and handed it to Smith, who read it and passed it to the others. It said:

MACLAREN CRASHED AT AKYAB, BURMA, PLANE COMPLETELY WRECKED—CONTINUANCE OF BRITISH FLIGHT DOUBTFUL.

Broome was devastated. The British had a spare plane north of Tokyo but it did not seem possible to deliver it to the marooned men. Smith said to the crushed Broome, "We'll get that machine to MacLaren somehow. Come up to Commander Abbott's bedroom and talk it over." John Abbott was the commander of the Destroyer Division in Japanese waters. They found Abbott in his pajamas and within five minutes worked out a practical plan for transporting the plane. In a short time, with the permission of Admiral Washington, commander of the United States Asiatic Fleet, they set up a relay of destroyers to deliver the aircraft to the stricken MacLaren. The common bonds of conquering the globe made better friends than enemies.

ABBOTT ARRANGED FOR the *Paul Jones* to take three big crates to Hong Kong where they were transferred to the *Preston* which took them to Akyab. The ever present Linton Wells, intrigued by world flights and world fliers, went along too.

At Akyab, the British plane, piloted by Flying Officer Plenderleith, had barely cleared the treetops on takeoff. Five minutes later, out of control, the plane dropped like a stone onto the water. The bottom of the hull smashed and the men had only an instant to get onto the tail before the nose submerged. Later MacLaren concluded that the mysterious accident had been caused by the torrential rains which had created over-expansion and sogginess in the aircraft after contraction from the heat of the Sind Desert. He was sure that continual exposure to extreme conditions was too much for the plane. Withstanding extreme temperatures was one of the great unknowns. One of the major American aims was to find out if aircraft could operate in various climates. Perhaps MacLaren's crash was a warning for them. They had survived the cold; soon they would find out if they could survive the heat. Some German air experts expressed fears that present day planes could not withstand the changes in climate from the Arctic to the Equator and used MacLaren's crash as an example.

MEANWHILE, THE AMERICAN fliers returned to Kasumigaura where the Japanese officers put them up at their club and in the evening gathered at the bar. Since the earthquake water was suspect, so they had a good excuse for drinking beer or whisky. The Japanese took turns keeping up with them. One evening a Japanese officer, in a spirit of friendliness, told Arnold that some day their two countries would be at war but that it would not be anything personal. His fellow officers overheard the remark and he quickly disappeared. Arnold never saw him again.

Life in Japan was not all social gatherings. There was, as usual, plenty of work and nobody except the crews ever touched the critical parts of the planes. They received outside help, but it was always incidental. If an engine was changed, they changed it. If the planes were washed, they washed them. They could not walk away from the planes after landing and leave them to ground crews like pilots of a later era. Each one was a mechanic. After overhauling the aircraft and installing larger radiators for the tropics, they were ready to go. One day before leaving, Smith made a test flight and took the commander of the naval base along as a passenger. Probably no gesture of good will meant more.

Things were looking brighter. They were sure, or thought they were sure, that the worst was over. June 1, the flight took off for Kushimoto down the coast. Crossing Yokohama Bay there was a clear view of the strikingly beautiful snow capped Mount Fujiyama that reached more than 12,000 feet into the sky. Before long, however, their affinity for bad weather was renewed. A rain storm they encountered turned into a mild typhoon. Fortunately, its strongest winds arrived after they landed.

The next day the flight arrived at the southern tip of Japan and two days later Smith received official command of the flight. As time had passed it had become increasingly impractical for Martin to rejoin the flight. In a gracious letter to Patrick, Martin wrote, "In fairness to Lt. Smith who succeeded me in command, I think he should so continue and himself bring the flight back to the United States . . . and I hope to join in welcoming him and the other fliers when the flight is ended." Like most noble gestures, it was also heart breaking. Nevertheless, Smith had been severely tested and he had met the test. He deserved nothing less than the recognition he received. From Japan onward the flight was his.

Smith must have appreciated the expression of confidence in receiving the command, but at the moment there appeared to be a hex on flight commanders. The *Boston* and *New Orleans* were on their way to Shanghai while the *Chicago* was left behind. The heavy plane refused to rise in the quiet water. It was a problem that they all faced at one time or another. The pontoons soaked up water that added weight. This time a loose strip of metal on one of the pontoons created extra resistance. Smith signaled to the others to proceed without him to prevent them from risking another takeoff.

The flight to Shanghai over a 550 mile open stretch of water where the Yellow Sea joined the East China Sea now became a new long distance sea hop. Destroyers of the 36th Division formed a radio chain along the line of flight. The first ship they passed was the loyal *Ford*. Now the weather was the best since leaving Santa Monica and for a change the journey was uneventful.

Crowds lined the banks of the Yangtze River at Shanghai and houseboats, tenders, launches and junks crammed the waters as part of the reception. It was a wonder that Wade and Nelson did not have a collision as they landed in the strong ebb tide. Lawton, the advance officer, and the harbor master had cleared a large landing area to avoid a crack-up; otherwise, landing would have been impossible. The Chief of the small Chinese Air Force, General Lee, and hordes of American residents greeted them. The flight was now in the Third Division and North America and Asia were linked by air.

A FEW DAYS before, d'Oisy, the French pilot, landed on the Kiangwan golf course and ran into a ditch that wrecked his plane. Lu Yung-hyang, Governor of Chekiang, loaned him another Breguet biplane and he continued on his way.

The American fliers stayed at the Hotel Astor in Shanghai and it was good to see so many people from their own country. Smith joined them the next day after making some minor repairs. There he learned the good news that Ogden had been promoted to Second Lieutenant. It was well deserved and, as an extra plus, a big help at diplomatic receptions. They were all lieutenants now. Shanghai was an exotic international city and some of them escaped for a while to see the night life. But the pressure was always there to keep moving. Two days after Smith landed, they were in the air again.

The next stop was Amoy on the Chinese coast. The original idea was to fly non-stop from Shanghai to Amoy, but now it seemed safer to make an intermediate stop at Tchinkoen Bay to refuel. The heat and light air made it wise to lighten their load. Politics as well as geography influenced the line of flight. China, supposedly an independent nation, was practically a protectorate of the European powers. Weakened by civil wars, the country was close to chaos. Warlords seized provinces, the north and south fought each other and everyone flouted the government at Peking. In Canton, the Kuomintang controlled a nationalist government that had sprung from revolutionaries who had rallied under the leadership of Sun Yat-sen. Entanglements in local politics would have been worse than a rough landing field.

Flying along the coast made sense for many reasons. There were numerous safe harbors and bulk plants of the Standard Oil Company of New York, a predecessor of the Mobil Oil Corporation, made a valuable link in the chain of supply. The Vacuum Oil Company, another Mobil predecessor, supplied the lubricating oil for the flight. The oil men were always anxious to help and Lawton named some of them local advance agents. At Hong Kong, J. W. Shaw, a Standard Oil employee, found a crane that was large enough to lift the *Chicago* onto a wharf so that its leaking pontoon could be replaced. A destroyer had brought a new pontoon from Tokyo. At the same time, a leaking cylinder jacket was welded.

Farther south, at Haiphong, the Governor gave a big reception to celebrate the first landing of the flight in French territory. The next day, June 11, the three planes failed to take off from the river at Haiphong because of light air and lack of wind. Finally, they taxied to the mouth of the river to find sufficient air and got off shortly before noon. This was only a minor delay. Actually they were pleased to be making up lost time. Things were moving now and they were making up for their frustrating Alaskan experiences.

Moments of confidence are often a time to beware. The brief interval of smooth sailing was abruptly interrupted on the way to Tourane, now known as Da Nang. The radiator on the *Chicago* overheated and Smith landed in a jungle lagoon to refill the water with their canvas bucket while the *Boston* and *New Orleans* circled above. The Liberty engine operated best when the water temperature was between 167° and 185° Fahrenheit. In about five minutes the *Chicago* was in the air again, but not for long. The radiator soon sprung a leak, water splashed into the cockpit and the red hot engine was in danger of bursting into flames. One of the cylinders cracked and the engine froze solid. As they landed in another lagoon in the middle of the jungle, a connecting rod punched a hole in the crankcase. Wade later recalled that during the *Chicago*'s approach it sounded like the engine was going to part company with the airplane—which it did, just before splashdown. Pistons, valves and rods exploded in all directions, proving the internal

In Haiphong harbor, sampans brought out the fuel and supplies the fliers needed.

combustion engine had its limitations for air travel. The other two planes landed beside the *Chicago*, held a quick conference, gave Smith and Arnold drinking water and then left for Tourane to make arrangements for a new engine.

While waiting for help, a native with impressive black teeth appeared in a dugout and excitedly gestured to them. Eventually the message got through that they had tangled their plane in one of his fishing traps. They got themselves loose and floated a short distance away. Two more natives arrived to take a look at this curiosity and then along came three Eurasian priests who spoke French. Arnold told them in his bad French that they needed food and water. The priests led him a few miles into the jungle to a village on stilts where there was a little church. They gave Arnold a glass of sacramental wine and a bottle of the wine to take back with him. Arnold thought the poor little church needed help as much as he did and he generously donated 50 dollars. It must have seemed like a fortune to the priests. That night Smith and Arnold slept on the wings of the plane.

At Tourane, a Monsieur Chevalier, one of the Standard Oil men that Lawton had designated as an advance agent, drove Nelson through the jungle on a military road in search of the downed fliers. At 2 A.M., Smith and Arnold heard paddles, and out of the darkness came a Swedish voice. It was Nelson and Chevalier with sandwiches and beer on ice. Nelson told them that he had made arrangements with the local tribe to tow them up river 15 miles to Hue, capital of Annam.

En route to Hue it was a matter of viewpoint as to who made the stranger sight, the Americans or natives. Gleeful native children, thrilled by the exciting arrival from another world, ran along the shore as sampans towed the plane. The native sampans had ten sparsely clothed paddlers. In the lead boat a patriarch beat a tom-tom. The chieftain sat under a sun shade with his favorite wives fanning him while his junior wives paddled. The aviators, more prosaic, stayed in the shade under the wings of the plane.

A Navy destroyer rushed at full speed with a new engine from Saigon to Tourane. Ogden drew the assignment to truck the 840-pound engine from Tourane to Hue. He would have preferred flying to the hair raising ride over the swampy, rutted jungle road. At Langco lagoon the truck drove onto a raft and started to sink. Luckily, the Vietnamese driver backed off without an instant to spare and waited for a larger raft.

The reason for going to Hue was that a bridge spanned the river

Here, Lt. Smith is taxiing to check out his mechanic's latest engine work.

there. Rigging a block and tackle on the bridge, they lifted the old engine out and dropped in the new one. It was hot, hard work. They rose at daybreak, but by ten in the morning the heat was almost unbearable. When they laid down a tool for a minute the sun would make it too hot to pick up. The metal parts of the plane were scorching hot, too. They became weak and queasy and gave up for a while. Arnold wrote, "I'm sure God never meant it to be as hot as it was here today." Still, 71 hours after their forced landing, the plane was ready for flight. They flew to Tourane in 40 minutes and landed in a beautiful harbor where Lawton had made excellent arrangements.

It was a relief to be on the move again. Besides, newspapers reported new competition for them. Portuguese world fliers, Major Brito Paes and Sarmento de Beines, had reached Bangkok.

On June 16, the Americans arrived in Saigon. The city, once occupied by Cambodians and then by Annamese, was now dominated by the French. Situated on the right bank of the Saigon River, the double rows of shady trees along the streets and the attractive gardens and museums made it one of the most beautiful places in the Far East. Linked by canals to the lower Mekong and by rail to Phnom Penh and Hanoi, it was the leading industrial center in Indo-China.

The Governor General invited the fliers to dinner but they had no clothes except overalls and sneakers. The Navy had been a big help along the way. Now they came to the rescue again with ready-made clothes. The Army men simply stood alongside a naval officer about the same size and borrowed his uniform. Decked out in white shirts and trousers, they took a boat to the dock and boarded the rickshas that they presumed were to take them to the palace. After some distance they became suspicious of their drivers. With the help of a passing Frenchman they learned that the ricksha drivers had figured, "American sailors—sporting house." They arrived late for dinner, but the Governor General enjoyed the story.

At Saigon it was decided to make an extra stop for fuel at Kampongsong Bay en route to Bangkok. The light air and soft water had given them too much trouble taking off all along the coast, so they lightened the load for shorter hops. The diminished density of the atmosphere in the torrid zone did not give them the needed lift to take off fully loaded. The change took a day to set up. Although it was a loss of valuable time, everyone agreed that it was better to relieve the motors of unnecessary strain.

The American planes were sighted over Saigon, June 16th, 1924.

When they reached Bangkok, capital of Siam, it was easy to see that a flight across the Malay Peninsula, instead of around it, would save about two days. The pontoons were still on the planes and over the jungle they would be out of gliding distance from water much of the time. After a brief conference, all six voted thumbs up for the risky route. They plotted the crossing and planned a rendezvous with an American destroyer near an island in the Andaman Sea. Lawton was with them and he helped finalize the details as he had all along the Third Division line of flight. A delay of one day allowed the destroyer to sail around the peninsula into Tavoy Bay where it would set up a temporary fueling base.

King Rama VI, the absolute monarch of Siam, was out of town. His representatives took charge of the reception and did their best to entertain their visitors. The most impressive sight in a fast half-day of sightseeing amidst canals and teakwood houses must have been the royal white elephants at the palace. Meeting a Siamese prince in his drawing room, they were surprised to see a photograph of Billy Mitchell. The General and his new wife had been there not long before on their tiger hunt.

On the flight to Tavoy, the clouds were low, and passing over a 4000-foot mountain the *New Orleans* had been caught in a downdraft and had a few tense minutes regaining altitude. Aside from that brief encounter, there were no difficulties. They reached Tavoy safely, refueled from the destroyer *Sicard*, and continued north to Rangoon, Burma, which was then a part of India.

In the crowded Rangoon River, a native sampan loaded with freight crashed into the lower right wing of the *New Orleans* while it was moored at Monkey Point, and caused five days delay. Nelson made the repairs with the intention of replacing the wing at Calcutta. Probably worse than a damaged wing was the dysentery that Smith picked up from the drinking water furnished by the natives at Hue. At least their troubles were well timed. While Smith recovered from the worst of his ailment, Nelson repaired his ship. The dangers of the Aleutians were behind them, but the tropics presented their own special problems. It was discouraging. Still, the Portuguese fliers were worse off. They reached Macao only to wreck their plane while taking off.

This American destroyer was awaiting the fliers in Saigon harbor with a full stock of spares.

When the flight arrived in Bangkok on June 18, Standard Oil employees were there ready to refuel them. American companies were a help to the flight all the way round the world.

A closer look at one of the D-WCs in the water.

VI

TO THE
MIDDLE EAST

STUART MACLAREN, waiting out the weather in a protected cove along the Burmese coast, heard the roar of planes passing overhead. Quickly looking up, he caught a glimpse of the three American biplanes headed toward Akyab. Both expeditions had hoped to meet somewhere in Burma to exchange pleasantries and compare experiences, but their timing was a little off. It would have to wait for another time.

Anxious to beat the bad weather, the World Cruisers took off from Akyab as soon as possible in a heavy rainstorm and passed through a number of "small" typhoons before they reached Chittagong, now in Bangladesh, for refueling. The monsoon season that they had hoped to avoid had already begun. Time was more important than ever if they wanted to escape the worst of the season. A few minutes after noon they set out for Calcutta, a commercial port in northeast India where ocean, river and rail traffic converged. Approaching the heavily populated city, the three planes descended in a line low over the palms and made a smooth landing on the Ganges River where multitudes gathered on the banks in the sweltering heat to see the unusual sight. It was a mystery to most of them since they had never even heard of the world flight.

Although the imperial grip on India had weakened, the British were still regarded as the rulers. Nevertheless, nationalism was on the rise. To stem the tide, the government had given added responsibilities to Indian officials in the hope that it would dilute the influence of Mahatma Gandhi, a little Hindu lawyer. Lord Reading, the viceroy, had some success in relaxing tensions while the natives prepared for greater struggles ahead. In 1924, the British, still hoping to keep their lines of communication open from the Indian Ocean through the Middle East to Great Britain, fought a delaying political action.

Smith, as commander, drew a handsome suite for himself at the fashionable Great Eastern Hotel. The luxury was too much. He invited Arnold to share his privileged quarters with him. While in Calcutta it might have been fun to enjoy the social gatherings of the

British imperialists in their declining days of glory, but the monsoons were too much on their minds. Under pressure, they postponed a change of motors as planned because it would take two more days. Instead, they shipped the engines by rail to Karachi, which was east of the monsoon belt. They would make the change there.

Now halfway around the world, they rushed not only to beat the monsoons, but also to make up lost time. Down river at Prinseps-bhat a crane hoisted the aircraft out of the water to remove the pontoons and mount wheels. This was a big occasion and hordes gathered to watch the ritual. It was a relief to the aviators to see the pontoons replaced because they would now have a lighter load and could develop greater speed. Nelson had expected to change the wing that had been damaged in the Rangoon River. Instead he found that his repairs were so good a change was unnecessary. More hours were saved.

William Jenkins, the American Consul at Calcutta, noticed that the modest manner and quiet attitude of the fliers impressed important elements of the British community who were prone to look upon all Americans as too boastful. These men did not fit the mold of the boisterous American male that the British had formed in their minds. Husband E. Kimmel, the highly regarded commander of Destroyer Division 45, also believed that the especially warm welcome at Rangoon and Calcutta had been influenced by the help that had been given to MacLaren. He thought the good sportsmanship had appealed to all classes of Britishers.

Still, Smith's bad luck persisted. Dysentery had seriously weakened him and he had lost a lot of weight. Now he fell into a hole and fractured his right floating rib. He reported the fractured rib to Patrick and then had a second thought for clarification. He added a postscript to his message that read, "The fall and resulting injury refers to Lt. Smith in person, not to plane." It probably came as some relief to Patrick. Although the accident did not hold up the departure for Allahabad, the slightest movement was painful for Smith and in the air the plane's rolling was sheer torture.

At Calcutta the fliers ran into the ubiquitous Linton Wells again. As always, he was busy looking for a story. Wells had no shortage of nerve and may have suggested that he fly to Allahabad with them. Weight was no problem since he was only 140 pounds and they had just shed the heavy pontoons. According to Wells, however, it was Wade who first suggested that he join them. Wells had been ordered

Lt. Smith and the *Chicago* as they prepared to discard the pontoons.

back to Tokyo by his office and one night said to Wade, "Well, here's where I leave you fellows. Back to Tokyo for me." He claimed that Wade answered, "Tell you what, if Lowell's agreeable, I'll take you along with me." Wells jumped at the chance for more excitement. The Richard Harding Davis days of adventurous newspapermen were far from over. At Paramushiru, Wells had asked Wade for a ride south but it was passed off with the reply that it would be a "damned cold ride." Now he had his big opportunity.

Wells went to Smith and said, "Lowell, Leigh's willing to take me along in Plane Three if you're agreeable." Smith had his doubts. It was true that publicity-conscious Air Service officers had given free rides to newspapermen at home, but not when they were trying to set a record. An unofficial passenger was risky business. Still, risks were their business and this seemed like only a mild amusement. And Wells must have been unusually persuasive. Finally, Smith agreed to cable Patrick for approval but he knew better than anyone that there would be no time to receive a reply.

When the flight was ready to take off no word had arrived from Patrick. Wells asked, "How about it, Lowell?" He answered, "Get your stuff together." Perhaps Smith tired of being the remote commander. This could be a way to break some of the tension among the men. Whatever the reason, Wells lost no time in writing and signing waivers absolving members of the flight from responsibility in case anything happened and was ready to go. If anything did happen they would need more than waivers.

Wade asked Ogden if Wells could share the seat in his cockpit and Ogden replied, "Suits me." For the next six and a half hours the two men were jammed together in the small space without an inch to spare. It was extremely uncomfortable, but Ogden never complained. The dispositions of the mechanics on the world flight were really out of this world. They took everything that came along in stride.

At Allahabad, the fliers took pleasure in putting Wells to work as payment for his ride. They gave him the job of refueling the three planes in the broiling sun. It meant sitting on top of the hot metal engine cowling and emptying one two-gallon can of gasoline after another into a chamois-covered funnel. He also added engine oil and cleaned the fuselage. Wells did the job and showed that he could take things in stride too, but he admitted that he had never worked so hard in his life.

While waiting for an answer from Patrick, Wells flew with them to Ambala, the principal operational base for the Royal Air Force on the Indian frontier, and then to Multan and Karachi, a port on the Arabian Sea which was then a part of India. Wade suggested to Ogden and Wells that they place a board on the arms of the seat to give themselves more room in the cockpit. It gave them about eight inches more width, but it was not the perfect solution to their problems. Now their heads were above the visor on the fuselage and their faces were badly wind-burned.

The *New Orleans* had developed a leak in the cylinder jacket and the British had sent a replacement to Ambala from their repair and supply depot at Lahore. To prevent any delay in their departure, Nelson and Harding began work at 3 A.M. to replace the cracked cylinder. At 9:20 A.M. they were ready to leave with the others for Multan.

Over the edge of the Sind Desert en route to Multan the flight ran into a nasty dust storm and the pilots attempted to fly over it. After reaching 5000 feet they realized that it was useless and descended to just above the ground. There was so little visibility it was like flying through fog.

Ogden and Wells, still seated above the fuselage, received the full blast of sand. It filled their eyes, ears, noses and mouths. Goggles were no help because the heat and dust obliterated their sight and they had to take them off. Their faces were as red as lobsters, lips dry and cracked, eyes bloodshot and their eyelids bleeding along the eyelashes. The temperature in the cockpit was 156° and the water in the extra-large tropical radiator boiled. Without the large radiators that had been installed in Tokyo they would have been in serious trouble.

Wells gave full credit to Wade's delicate sense of touch in handling a plane, and Nelson's mechanical ability, but he thought Smith's navigation was nothing short of miraculous. He said Smith had the instincts of a homing pigeon. With simple instruments, charts that were not much more detailed than maps in an atlas, and landmarks covered by sand, he still led from point to point without losing the way.

Landing at Multan, a city with a hostile population of Moslems and Hindus, the temperature was 116° in the shade and remained nearly the same all night. The experts had wondered if a plane had been built to withstand the extreme changes in climate. The World Cruisers were passing the test. So far, from the northern Pacific to southern Asia,

Lt. Smith and the *Chicago* back on wheels and dry land.

they had taken unbelievable stress and kept on flying. The heat, however, had an effect upon the men. It was difficult to rest and Smith, under considerable strain himself, noticed the effects on each of the men. Hot and tired, it was hard to think straight. The flight was now a battle of endurance. Flier fatigue challenged the Liberty engine and the weather for top place on the long list of menaces to success.

During the last hundred miles to Karachi the desert was completely uninhabited and in this rough terrain it would be almost impossible to make a forced landing without destroying the plane and perhaps the crew. Over this broad expanse, about 55 miles from Karachi, the *New Orleans'* engine went bad, probably because of sand. One of the valves came loose and dropped down in the cylinder. That caused the piston and connecting rod to break, and the valve head dropped through, creating three large holes in the lower half of the crankcase. The rocker arm tappet also broke. The plane, literally covered in oil, continued to run but there was danger of fire at any minute. Oddly, the engine kept running even when it had no reason to run. It lost about 200 rpm, but eleven cylinders chugged away. Nelson thought the connecting rod must have stuck in the top of the cylinder. A forced landing was imminent.

The trouble had begun at an altitude of about 5000 feet. Nelson lost about 100 feet and then he glided off at an angle of 45 degrees from course, let the wind carry him upward, then slid off at 45 degrees in the other direction, came up as far as he could and repeated the same maneuver. When he lost too much altitude, he gunned the engine which rumbled, sputtered, smoked and, miraculously, kept chugging along.

While Nelson struggled with the *New Orleans*, Wade circled, looking for a possible landing area in this impossible country, and Smith held the course. Everyone expected the worst at any moment. The moments dragged on and to their surprise the worst did not happen. Somehow Nelson managed to reach Karachi on the eleven cylinders. After landing he found the head of the valve in the engine cowling but he never learned exactly what caused the trouble.

Wells had watched the whole incident from the cockpit of the *Boston*. Always the reporter, he asked Harding what he was doing while Nelson battled to stay in the air. Harding said, "Well, for a time I sang 'Nearer My God to Thee' and then I changed to 'Jesus Savior

Pilot Me.'" Hearing the remark, Nelson said, "First time I've ever been called Jesus."

Karachi was the Royal Air Force supply and repair depot for all air service activities in India. It was also the city included on all routes laid out for world flights and as a result the Americans were welcomed as a curiosity because they flew west instead of east. Throughout the journey they had fought the westerlies. By now, Nelson was convinced that they would have saved two months if they had flown eastward. He may have been right, but while the British had crashed, the French had crashed and the Portuguese had crashed, the Americans were still going.

Working 16 hours a day, all engines were replaced within two days. The RAF did all they could to help and the proper equipment made the job a lot easier. Sun helmets and shorts, unknown in American Army attire, were major contributions by the British. It helped keep the Americans cool, but there was a drawback. Everyone ended up with sunburned knees.

The fliers still did the critical work themselves and the primitive ground facilities were one of the great challenges of the flight. Four hours sleep was now looked upon as more or less normal. After arriving at a destination they continued to follow a routine procedure of plane maintenance that took up to three hours. They lived with the engines, fuel system and water system. The Liberty engine had lots of plumbing and the potential for trouble was enormous. Nelson said that it was usually the small things that let them down. Oil leaks from different joints of the engine caused hours of extra work. Sometimes the oil covered the planes from engine to rudder. Leaks in crankcase joints, the cylinder hold-down flanges and camshaft housing were all the result of careless assembling. Sometimes a few minutes could correct the trouble; more often it would take many tedious hours. If the engines had been carefully assembled in the first place, hours and hours could have been saved. When a pilot or mechanic finished work on his plane he would lend the others a hand. Refueling was a slow process too because, as Linton Wells found out, every gallon passed through a chamois to insure that no water or grit got into the fuel tank.

By now, Wells had reached the end of his ride. At Karachi a terse message from Washington forbade his continued presence on the journey. Sweating out the long flight at home, it is not difficult to imagine

The six fliers in Baghdad, Persia.

the exasperation in General Patrick's office. Wells, in a delayed reaction, worried about Wade and Smith being court martialed. It was a little late for such worries. Fortunately, the fear was unnecessary. The Allahabad correspondent for Reuters News Agency filed a story that there was a stowaway in the fuselage baggage compartment. It was a story that stuck as far as the public was concerned and would be repeated time and again for years to come. Perhaps it helped protect the fliers from the wrath of higher ups, but it is highly unlikely that Patrick or the Air Staff were taken in by such a far-fetched tale. They might not care for carrying newsmen on a world flight, but they had to admit that giving the press a lift in the United States was not uncommon. At any rate, nothing came of the episode.

Wells received a message from his boss through the American consul at Karachi about the same time telling him that he had been fired for not returning to Tokyo. Wells, a free spirit, had even more freedom now. However, he would not have traded the experience with the world flight for his job and the loss did not seem to worry him. In the twenties and thirties he would become well known to the American public for his roving correspondent stories.

On the way to Baghdad, Mesopotamia, the city of the Arabian nights, stops were made at Chahbar, Bandar Abbas and Bushire, Persia. At Bandar Abbas, where the Gulf of Oman and the Persian Gulf join, the British Consul, a Mr. Richardson, acted as their advance agent. No one thought that it was the least unusual that a representative of a country with an entry in the world flight sweepstakes should handle American affairs. He was especially helpful in improving the rolling, irregular airstrip on the beach east of town before they landed. Since there was a cholera epidemic the Consul had the fliers as guests in his home so that they would avoid the heavily populated part of the town where chances of coming down with the disease were much greater.

The landing field at Bushire was a station on the airway from Baghdad to Karachi. Halverson, the advance officer for the Fourth Division, made the necessary arrangements shortly before the arrival of the flight and then left for Baghdad. The traveling conditions, poor facilities and poor communications gave him plenty to worry about in this remote area. Always conscientious, he did everything possible to smooth the way for the flight. In hot, humid Calcutta he had picked up malaria and ran a fever that sapped his energy. Yet he kept up with all of the details as he moved from one station to another. The job came first and his health second. If he could help it, no one would say that he let down the flight as they moved through the Middle East. As he contended with disease and desolation he overlooked nothing. He was an experienced pilot and he knew what the fliers needed.

On July 8, the flight took off from Bandar Abbas at 5:40 A.M. Up at 3:30 A.M., they refueled the planes from about 100 two-gallon tins. Things were running smoothly again and their speed since leaving Calcutta elated them. Eager for an early start, some of the fliers missed breakfast, and sandwiches for lunch did not arrive in time. Despite all of their careful preparations, food in the air never had a high priority in their plans. No one worried about eating well; sandwiches were good enough.

Following the coastline because of high mountains inland, they passed few emergency landing areas on the first part of the flight. Later, beyond the Mund River, the country was more populated and there were some cultivated sections. At 9:30 A.M. they arrived at Bushire, a port on the Persian Gulf, for a quick stop to refuel. They found the field which had been built by the French in excellent condition and there was even a partially completed hangar and several planes.

George Fuller, the American Vice Consul at Bushire, noticed the difference in the advance arrangements made for each of the world flights. The Portuguese waited three days for supplies and permission from Teheran to leave Persia. The Frenchman d'Oisy had to spend the night. The British MacLaren required three hours for one machine. The Americans took about an hour and a half to load oil, water and gasoline and go on their way. The flight was now a day ahead of schedule. Fuller wished they could have stayed longer.

Leaving Bushire, the pilots followed the coast to a point near Bandar Dilan and then took a compass course over desert to Basra. They passed over an emergency field at Basra and followed the Euphrates River, a birthplace of western civilization, to Hilla where they took a direct compass course to Baghdad. The desert was uninhabited, but the weather was ideal. The hungry, weary men ate their dinner at 10 P.M. Arnold remembered getting into bed, but he did not remember lying down.

Baghdad, the centuries old crossroads for caravans in southwest Asia, was the RAF headquarters that controlled Mesopotamia. In World War I, an Anglo-Indian force occupied most of the country, and in 1920 Great Britain received a mandate over the area. In 1922, the

British recognized the independent kingdom of Iraq, but their influence remained. The troop-carrying planes of 8 Squadron, RAF, were used to combat raiding parties of natives. Since 1921 the city was also an active air center because the RAF had inaugurated a weekly air mail service to Cairo. The route crossed the Suez Canal and the northern end of the Dead Sea to Ziga. After a refueling stop, the mail route continued over desert to Ramadi and then to Baghdad. The Douglas World Cruisers intrigued the RAF engineering officers who were surprised to find them in such good condition after so many hardships.

On July 10, the flight arrived in Constantinople, Turkey, via Aleppo, the ancient city that was the center of the Hittites before 1000 B.C. It was now the hub of aviation activity for the French in mandated Syria. The day before they had flown up the Euphrates Valley to Dier-ez-Zor to Muslimieh Airdrome north of Aleppo, a key station for the French Air Service in the Levant. Along the way there were many emergency landing fields that were used regularly by the French on their airway mission.

Flying to Constantinople was almost entirely over mountains, which required "considerable high altitude work." The high altitudes were about 7000 feet. Smith told about flying through one canyon that was so narrow the wing tips almost touched the towering walls. Below them were wild torrents and above them were thick clouds. It was a little too close for comfort. Part of the way the tracks of the Berlin-Baghdad railroad, which ran through the Bulgar Mountains, were a big help in keeping on the right course. Skipping a planned stop at Konia in south central Turkey, they completed two sections of the flight in one day. Now they were at the threshold of Europe.

The airfield at Constantinople was large and in fairly good condition. A number of French mechanics were working there to make it a terminal for an airline from Paris. The French efforts, however, would be in vain. The Turkish government, intent upon modernizing itself, was still suspicious of the western nations it was trying so hard to imitate. When the French completed the landing field, the Turks changed their minds and decided to keep out foreigners.

Turkey was now a Sultan-less republic moving into the modern world. Changes were evident everywhere. Mustapha Kemal, the new leader, made the western alphabet mandatory, established polygamy as a criminal offense, and brought women out of the harem. Unveiled women, a sharp departure from ancient custom, appeared everywhere.

There were still some streetcars with separate compartments for women but they were not used much.

Good guesswork rather than good communications prompted Halverson, advance officer for the Fifth Division Wash and the American High Commissioner, Admiral Mark Bristol, to go out to the airfield on the off chance that the flight might show up. The Admiral's interest was more than routine. In 1913, he had served as an energetic head of the new Office of Naval Aeronautics. His slogan had been, "Take the Air Service to Sea." The following year he established an air station at Pensacola, Florida, for the Navy's nine planes, six qualified commissioned pilots and 23 enlisted men.

None of the late wires had arrived so there was no exact information. For Halverson this was the last stop in the Fourth Division and his work was almost over. Still suffering with a high fever, he would be glad to turn over the responsibility for advance work. Wash said that he had seldom seen a more conscientious and industrious officer than Halverson, who had been working night and day under adverse conditions. The considerate Wash generously mentioned Halverson's dedication to duty in his final report because he was quite sure that Halverson would omit any reference to his illness.

While the men stood aimlessly around the airport, the flight appeared. Since no one had really expected them, none of the Turkish officials were present, but later in the afternoon Smith met the Chief of Air Service and the Commanding General of their armies. Smith also noticed Halverson's poor health and would give him credit for operating under a large handicap in his own report. Actually, Smith, still recovering from his broken rib, was none too healthy himself.

Constantinople turned out to be fun. They had dinner at a cabaret and relaxed a little. After weeks of suffocating heat and near exhaustion they needed it, but they were really keen on continuing the flight while things were going well. Nevertheless, the Turkish officials requested that they remain another day to show them their planes and equipment. This did not please them since there was no other reason to remain. Admiral Bristol advised them to wait because the inspection was an agreed upon condition to gain the reluctantly granted permission to fly through Turkey. Wash was glad to see the delay because he thought all the fliers needed rest, especially Smith, who appeared very tired.

VII

ACROSS EUROPE

WHEN WASH arrived in Constantinople he hired a stenographer and worked for ten straight days preparing references for the flight across Europe. He had inspected every airfield, including emergency fields, checked gasoline and oil quality, workshops, weather services and mechanics. He also arranged for hotels, transportation, guards, interpreters and a hundred other details. Then he boiled down the vital information. He carefully compiled route descriptions, plotted emergency fields on maps and made sketches of airdromes. Sections were subdivided and exhibits numbered and indexed to correspond with the report so that information could be found easily. Each pilot would receive a separate dossier. Wash's efficiency was probably one reason he would become the youngest general officer in the Army by 1941. During World War II, Wash learned that he was to be given command of the Eighth Air Force in England and tragically was killed in an air crash the same day.

When Smith arrived, Wash turned over the data to him and then took the Orient Express to Paris so that he would be on hand when they landed.

Flying over Bulgaria on the first leg across the continent, the fliers landed at the eastern terminal of the Compagnie Franco-Roumaine de Navigation Aérienne in Bucharest, Rumania, where once more they took everyone by surprise. No one had even heard that the flight had reached Constantinople. Smith simply telephoned the American Ambassador from the field to let him know that they had arrived. There were no problems. Bucharest impressed the world fliers even more than it had Wash. After the Middle East, it looked like a clean, "snappy" looking place with many well dressed, attractive girls. Unfortunately there was no time for sightseeing or meeting girls. Queen Marie, at her summer castle in Transylvania, invited them for the weekend, which would have been a pleasant interlude, but it was one more invitation they had to turn down.

At 6:00 A.M. the next morning they were off again. Free air passage across Europe was not yet an accepted practice. International air agreements were still to be worked out. During the past year, the Franco-Roumanian line had had twelve planes confiscated by Germany for flying over their territory. Germany justified her action by pointing out that France did not permit German planes over French soil. Only England, with greater foresight, welcomed airplanes of all nations. The world flight freely crossing borders without hindrance was something new.

At Belgrade, officials waited at Panchevo Airdrome where arrangements had been made for the arrival of the Americans. But since the weather was good, despite head winds, the flight kept going, much to the dismay and embarrassment of foreign service officers on the ground. In his diary, Harding still referred to the new nation of Yugoslavia as Serbia.

Moving rapidly, the fliers had lunch in Budapest and dinner in Vienna. Their arrival at Matyasfild Airdrome, Budapest, was still another surprise. Telegraphic communications in that part of the world were admittedly unreliable, but it was the confidential opinion of an American foreign service officer at the legation at Budapest that a garbled message had been intentionally sent from Bucharest to irritate the Hungarians. There was intense ill feeling between the two countries and it was believed that the Rumanians thought the lack of a reception in Hungary would place them in a bad light. Rumania, now double its pre-war size, had actually invaded Hungary. The allies had had their hands full trying to convince the Rumanians to leave. Such diplomatic maneuverings were of little interest to the fliers. After lunch, Harding was so interested in talking to a pretty girl he did not notice the others were ready to leave. "Come on, Johnny," one of them yelled.

Vienna, only a short time before a center of the Austro-Hungarian Empire of the Hapsburgs, was now part of a small republic. The fliers found the largest crowd of interested people at the airfield since leaving Japan, but all they wanted was gasoline, oil and sleep. Tired or not, their industry amazed the slower paced Austrians. The aim was to reach Paris the following day. It would be July 14, Bastille Day, a perfect day for celebration. The Viennese press gave the flight a friendly reception and one newspaperman noticed that though Nelson had said little, he did speak German. This pleased them. A foreign service officer thought that the best illustration of the high regard of the Austrians for the aviators was the fact that the exclusive Hotel Imperial charged only $1.40 per flier for the best rooms in the house.

Leaving Vienna at 5:50 A.M., the flight followed the picturesque Danube River part of the way. A quick stop was made at Strasbourg, France, for refueling and then they took off again. They followed commercial airways to Nancy where, despite their rush, they took a detour to the north over battlefields in the Saint Mihiel salient where aviation had played an important part in the American offensive only a few years before. In four days, American aviators had made 3300 flights over the lines and were in the air over 4000 hours. It was there that Frank Luke, the top ace of the American Air Service, became known as the "Balloon Buster" and in the last 17 days of his life shot down 18 enemy aircraft. These were fresh memories. Some of the countryside had been cultivated, with few traces of the war remaining, while other parts appeared as though fighting had just stopped.

About 100 miles east of Paris, two flights of French Army planes met them and escorted them to the city where the Americans circled the Arc de Triomphe as a gesture of respect. At 5:15 P.M. they landed at Le Bourget airfield. Even with their side trip over the battlefields they set a new record with their Tokyo to Paris flight. It was a day and a half better than the time set by Captain Pelletier d'Oisy from Paris to Tokyo with his two planes. Their speed through Europe was remarkable even to themselves. From Bucharest, Budapest, Vienna and Paris, Smith's reports to Patrick had the same refrain, "All OK."

Approaching Le Bourget in triangle formation, they were saluted by a parachute rocket in the cloudless skies and a huge crowd that swept past the police. All thoughts of an orderly reception ceased. So many people swarmed over the planes that the world fliers had to start the motors, taxi to a hangar and close the doors. Three years later Charles Lindbergh would have the same fears for his plane. Eventually they made their way to the airport office where newspapermen followed with dozens of questions.

The correspondent for the *London Times* described the fliers as bronzed and healthy, with the exception of the bronzed Smith who looked thin and weary. Nevertheless, he thought Smith was a "fine specimen of manhood with handsome features" who accepted congratulations with a becoming modesty and replied to questions in monosyllables.

The world flight becomes the toast of the Continent when they
get as far as France. Here, refueling in Strasbourg.

Smith had a question for the newspapermen. He asked how the Americans were doing in the Olympics that were being held near Paris that summer. The reporters answered that they were doing quite well. The day before, the United States had won the track and field events and broke two world records and one Olympic mark. This was the year that Johnny Weissmuller would win the 100 meter and 400 meter swimming races and Helen Wills would take the women's tennis singles, the first major triumph for an American woman tennis star in 17 years.

The French Under Secretary for Air, Laurent Eynac, welcomed the flight and said that he had watched their progress with interest, anguish and relief. Le Bourget was an eye opener for the American fliers. They could easily see the progress of commercial aviation. Planes busily arrived and departed from all over Europe. There was nothing like this in the United States.

Wade and Arnold, no strangers to Paris, did a little sightseeing on their own and drifted into a place in Montmarte. Somebody came over to them and pointed out that General Pershing was across the room. They said they had never been introduced and paid no more attention. Soon an aide came over and said that the General would like to see them. Pershing knew all about the flight and said that he was looking forward to having lunch with them the next day.

All of the fliers were invited to the Folies Bergere the first night. It was an invitation that they could not resist. The show was great, but the seats were too comfortable and all six fliers fell asleep. They had a good excuse. In 12 flying days they had traveled 6128 miles and had flown an average of seven hours a day. When they returned to their hotel a correspondent reported that their orders to the hotel staff were, "Don't disturb us before eleven o'clock on any pretext unless the hotel takes fire, and not even then unless the firemen say there is no hope."

The next day, after Smith placed a wreath on the Tomb of the Unknown Soldier, General Pershing entertained the fliers at lunch at Foyot's, President Doumergue held a reception at Elysee Palace, the Vice President of the Municipal Council had them sign "The Golden Book" of the City of Paris and the Aero Federation de France gave a dinner at the Interallied Club. The lieutenants found it a novel experience to receive so much attention from generals in one day.

Dinner ended early to give the men a chance to rest. But sometime during their brief stay they found time to explore some of the charms of Paris. Aside from dropping in on such night clubs as "The Dead Rat" and "The Nimble Rabbitt," they visited the Langer Restaurant on the Champs Elysee. Monsieur Langer, a wartime acquaintance of Wade's, kissed him on both cheeks and jubilantly celebrated the occasion by leading the orchestra himself. The overjoyed proprietor completely ignored his other customers, who did not seem to mind a bit.

The next day, July 16, the flight left for London. A Handley-Page commercial airplane that flew the London to Paris route slowed down its speed about 20 miles per hour and accompanied them on a pleasant three hour run. Handley-Page had begun regular flights between the two cities in 1919. Their planes, now a part of the new Imperial Airways, were considered among the largest, safest and most comfortable in the world. The company had first used reconverted bombers, but their W8, built in 1920, became the first aircraft built in Great Britain solely for civil transport. It had a crew of two and carried 12 passengers.

The Cruisers circled Croydon Airdrome in column formation and landed amidst another great crowd that included many American tourists. Among the greeters was Mrs. MacLaren, who wanted to thank them for helping her husband. This was an anxious time for her. That same day news arrived that the British flight was missing on the way to Paramushiru. All Britons were obviously distressed by the news, but it did not affect the warm welcome for the Americans.

It was a good year to visit Great Britain. The desolate years immediately following the war, described in T. S. Eliot's poem "The Waste Land," had passed. Mirage or not, there was a brief moment of prosperity and hope for the future. The employed worker was better off than ever before, Ramsay MacDonald headed the first Labour Government and the masses felt that their two great grievances, housing and unemployment, would soon be solved. London was a lively place and the changes in style created the image of a new world. Bobbed hair, short skirts, make-up and cigarettes molded the slightly shocking modern woman's image. Dancing, mixed drinks, fancy dress parties and the game of chasing clues were all the rage. Late hours at notorious nightclubs were popular with the smart set. And the Kit Kat Club, visited by the Prince of Wales, and "43" on Gerrard Street, patronized by Tallulah Bankhead, Herbert Marshall and the Crown Prince of Sweden, were among the more notorious of these.

Jazz in England meant a heavy beat of the drums, hooters and banjos. It differed from the sound of trumpets and the moaning of saxophones that were favorites in America. The Jog Trot and the Shimmy were soon to be replaced by the frenetic Charleston. The "bright young things" described that year by the new young playwright, Noel Coward, would have undoubtedly taken the handsome, young aviators into their circle if there had been time. But it is highly unlikely that the languid, self-indulgent sophisticates would have captured the fun-loving fliers for very long. They were complete opposites. Energy, hard work and living for goals, without the slightest sign of self-pity, were ingrained parts of the fliers' system.

One evening the fliers were guests of the British Air Ministry at dinner. In these dignified surroundings Wade fell asleep at the table. The Surgeon General of the RAF, sitting next to him, stood up and humorously pronounced him physically unfit and excused him from dinner. Everyone understood it was a big joke, but the weariness was real.

In the morning the flight went to Brough Airdrome, near Hull on the north shore of the Humber not far from the North Sea. Here preparations began for the dangerous Sixth Division. No one had ever flown across the Atlantic from east to west. In 1919, two Britishers, Major Wood and Captain Wyllie, had made an attempt that ended disastrously in the Irish Sea.

Smith, Arnold and Wade, from necessity rather than desire, returned to London for a banquet given by the Royal Aero Club of England. The Air Chief Marshall of the RAF and Ambassador William Kellogg were present, as well as many titled aristocrats who impressed the airmen with their good sportsmanship. News had just been received that MacLaren and his companions were safe and it brightened up the festivities. The Duke of Atholl, an aviation enthusiast, telegraphed the gathering, "We feel that they [the Americans] will join us in our joy and relief at MacLaren's safety." At the banquet, Lord Thomson, Secretary of State for Air, said, "In enterprises of such magnitude petty jealousies fade." The American Ambassador offered his prayers and good wishes for MacLaren, and Smith proposed a toast to the British flier saying, "True airmen worked for furthering aviation in the world and not for any one country or people." International goodwill filled the room.

Immediately following the banquet, the Prince of Wales received the American fliers in his apartment. The Prince was on his way to the United States and he proceeded to make bets with them that he would arrive first. He planned on taking the sleek Cunard liner, *Berengaria*, which would cross the ocean in a safe six days. They took him on, for the sum of one pound. Later, King George V and Queen Mary invited them to a garden party, but once again they turned down a royal invitation.

At Brough, the facilities of the Blackburn Aeroplane Company were made available for the World Cruisers. The company was one of the leaders of the British aviation industry. At the time, their major project was the construction of a monster bomber for the Air Ministry which was near completion. Called the "Cubaroo," it was the largest single-engine plane in the world with the highest powered aircraft engine ever built. The nine ton plane had a carrying capacity of three tons, a wing span of 88 feet, a length of 54 feet, and a height of 19 feet. There were two pairs of landing wheels and Messrs. D. Napier and Son had supplied the 1000 horsepower engine. In a few weeks it would be ready for its first test flight.

H. G. Bentley, the manager at Blackburn, said,

We simply admire and admire and admire these Americans. Their thoroughness and the fierce manner in which they attack the dirty work which they know must be done in connection with the refitting and adjusting of their machines is wonderful. Since they arrived here they literally have never taken off their overalls. Dinners have been given in their honor, and perhaps one or two have gone merely to represent the squadron. The rest have stayed behind. They wanted to continue the work on their machines which they knew must be done while they are here or not at all. I have never seen men take their work so seriously. They have not rushed in the slightest degree; but have planned their work methodically and have set about surmounting every difficulty that has presented itself. They, of course, have a good number of our men helping them, but they themselves are actually doing the work they know must be done perfectly.

The fliers looked at themselves differently. Compared with the strain they had undergone before, this seemed like mere loafing. With good equipment and help they changed engines in less than a day. By anyone else's standards, they put in six hard days. Smaller radiators were installed for the cold weather ahead, wheels came off, pontoons went on, minor repairs were made to the wings near the aileron hinges, compasses compensated and any number of odd jobs performed. Replacement wings were on hand but were not needed. A careful inspection showed that the original varnish was still in first class condition.

Even with good equipment, risks were ever present. One day while replacing landing gear with pontoons a crane lifted the *Chicago* onto a dolly while the men took turns working underneath. The plane hung in the air with a chain tested to take a strain of six and half tons. It was far more strength than was necessary and there was no reason to expect trouble. Nevertheless, shortly after completing the work, the chain broke and the plane crashed to the floor. A few minutes sooner and one or more of the men would have been killed. It was a narrow escape. The pontoons were ruined, but there was a spare set meant for the *Seattle*, so they started work all over again.

Major Howard C. Davidson, Assistant Military Attaché at London, was at Brough and he believed that the fliers' original enthusiasm for the flight had died out by the time they reached England. All that remained was their grim determination to see it through. The one exception, he said, was Harding. He was always cheerful and smiling and appeared to be just as enthusiastic as the day he started. The pilots were much more tired than the mechanics. Davidson wrote Patrick, "Smith was very serious and the responsibility of leading the expedition had undoubtedly been a heavy burden. This was probably augmented by the jealousy of the others at being led by a man their same age and rank. He was very sure of himself and asked no advice from the rest of them but he was very very tired."

Davidson's observations about the six men who were giving every ounce of energy to achieve their goal had a ring of truth. There's no doubt that they were tired, just as there's no doubt that any romantic ideas about the flight disappeared long ago. Smith had said publicly in London that he would not take the trip again for a million dollars. The only reason to make it this time was for "the sake of one's country." The remark may have sounded overly patriotic, yet it was true. None of the men expected personal fame or fortune. That had never been their motivation. First, they were aviators interested in air progress, especially American air progress. They were members of the Army Air Service, under orders, who hoped to build its world prestige. Finally, they were just men doing a job.

Now that the flight came closer to home and showed signs of success, newspapermen increased their coverage. Too many of them, though, wrote about the fliers as though they were Rover Boys on a lark. Correspondents stressed the rollicking adventure with little appreciation for the real problems and tensions. At times it seemed as though the flight would never end or end too quickly. Every day was a strain and any day might have been their last. The men did not even share their inner fears with each other. The monotonous jobs as well as the dangers were interminable and both took a toll on their nervous systems. By now they had been working closely together for eight months, had been away from home almost five strenuous months and still had a long way to go. The world flight was all consuming.

The flight had been as heavy a burden for Smith as it would have been for any man. The strain affected all of them, but Smith carried the extra load of command. He had more to worry about than himself or his plane. He had taken over a flight that was faltering, if not failing, at its most difficult time and met one challenge after another as the Pacific, Asia, the Middle East and Europe melted away. Time after time his judgment was proven right.

The wonder may be that these six men worked so well together under such pressure. This was an exclusive little group. They were good, brave, skillful men, but they were not perfect. Yet underneath any differences there was the common bond of the flight and a readiness to help each other regardless of risk to themselves. When all was said and done they were friends. It was a friendship that no one outside the flight could possibly understand fully. Now they faced another dangerous challenge in the Atlantic. There were other failures, but no precedents for them to follow. They were keyed up. Still, Smith knew that it was better for them to be keyed up than let down.

Smith heard reports of plans for elaborate receptions when they arrived in the United States. That was something he did not want. No one could ever claim that he was a glory seeker, but more than that was on his mind. He recommended to Patrick that no entertainment be arranged until the finish of the flight to reduce chances of damage to the planes and to prevent personnel from becoming relaxed. There was a flight to finish as quickly as possible. The time to relax would be after they landed in Seattle.

A news report from Amsterdam announced that Major Pedro Zanni would take off in a few days and follow MacLaren's route. Zanni, an Argentinian, would take off from Rotterdam on his third attempt to circle the world. This time he had a novel idea and was sure that he could catch up with his competitors. He planned to use three Fokker planes to complete the journey. First, he would use a land plane. At Calcutta, he would substitute a seaplane, and for the Atlantic he would fly a Fokker flying boat. The planes were noted for their speed and he was confident that the plan would work. About this time, Smith also learned that official arrangements had been cleared for Lieutenant Antonio Locatelli, an Italian aviator, to fly their route across the Atlantic and take advantage of any of their leftover supplies.

General Patrick cabled Smith to start from Brough when supplies were distributed along the route and Navy ships were in position. The Navy, as in the Pacific, had instructions to safeguard the flight, maintain a chain of communications and give all assistance. Their help was especially appreciated after the original plan to install a radio in one of the planes had been discarded.

In 1919, Lt. Commander Albert Read and his crew in the NC-4 had flown across the Atlantic from Rockaway, New York, to Newfoundland, the Azores, Lisbon and finally England. This southern route offered better weather, but the distances were long. From the Azores to Newfoundland was about 1400 miles. Another possibility was to fly from the Azores to Bermuda, but that distance was worse, about 2100 miles. The Army plan was to hazard the north Atlantic in the summertime and hope to avoid bad weather. They would fly over the Faeroes to Iceland, and then hop to Greenland, and then Labrador. The distances were shorter, but the key to success, as always, was the weather. No one wanted to face conditions similar to the Aleutians again.

On July 30, the flight left Brough for Kirkwall on Pomona, one of the larger islands in the Orkneys at the northern tip of Scotland. They were met by the cruiser USS *Richmond* and went aboard to confer with Rear Admiral Thomas P. Magruder about a system of cooperation based upon their Pacific and Asiatic experiences. They also checked the weather. Patrol boats reported heavy fog which forced them to delay departure to await better conditions.

With rare free time on their hands, the fliers took a small boat to view the remains of the sunken German fleet at nearby Scapa Flow. Seventy-four German ships, including 11 battleships, five battle cruisers and 50 destroyers had been interned by the British after the war. In 1919, after the Armistice, the German crews had succeeded in scuttling all except four of the large ships and a few destroyers. Embarrassed by the trickery, the British undertook mammoth plans for raising the ships and salvage operations were now underway. The first ship, a destroyer, would be brought to the surface within the next two days. As the Americans viewed the ghostly scene, a British naval coast plane overhead sent a semaphore, "Good luck from British Air Service."

Smith even found time for a round of golf with Major Davidson against Captain Cotton and Commander Keppler of the *Richmond*. He rarely played golf, but he was so well coordinated he played almost like an expert. Nevertheless, the Navy won on Cotton's long putt on the 18th hole.

VIII

THE NORTH ATLANTIC

ON AUGUST 2, the sun was shining, the sky was clear and the flight started for Iceland. Again, there was trouble taking off because there was no wind. Again, Wade came to the rescue by dropping down dangerously close in front of the *Chicago* to create rough water and sufficient air currents. A less skillful pilot would have surely crashed. An hour had been lost and before long they found themselves in fog. The planes climbed above the fog where they continued on course for about 30 minutes when they found themselves trapped in heavier fog. Nelson said the visibility was "about six inches." Smith and Wade, using their simple instruments, climbed and turned back out of the fog, coming out at an altitude of 2800 feet, where they circled for about a half hour looking for Nelson. Fearing that the *New Orleans* had had an accident, the *Chicago* and *Boston* returned to Kirkwall and dropped a message at the hotel before they landed. It read:

SEND A MESSAGE TO THE RICHMOND THAT WE ALL BECAME SEPARATED IN THE FOG AND THAT WADE AND I HAVE NOT SEEN NELSON SINCE WE BECAME SEPARATED ON THE COURSE TWENTY-FIVE MILES FROM BIRSAY.

Nelson had come in close contact with backwash air that threw him into a partially out of control nose dive. Finding himself in a high-speed spiral, he closed the throttle, braced himself against the back of his seat and centered the turn needle with the rudder-bar. Cautiously coming back on the wheel, he pulled out just in time to drop through a hole of clear air and open space in the fog about ten or 15 feet above water. Flattening out, he thought the others were above him. He went up into the clouds again and broke out on top of them. Equally concerned about Smith and Wade, he flew over the destroyer *Billingsley* and dropped a message to the deck:

IF PLANES 2 AND 3 HAVE PASSED BLOW TWO BLASTS ON WHISTLE, IF NOT BLOW ONE.

Lt. Nelson flew on alone.

The *Billingsley* responded with a single blast. Nelson, with one objective impressed on his mind, decided to keep going and followed a compass course to Iceland although his oil pressure dropped from 60 to 27 pounds and the engine was running rough. He flew above the fog part of the way and, by reading the angle of the celestial bodies with a sextant, he made accurate locations on the Great Circle and found his way to Hoefn Hornafjord, Iceland, at 3:40 P.M. The *New Orleans* was the first aircraft to ever reach Iceland and it was a big thrill for all the villagers. Nelson, in his decompressed manner, said, "The flight was all right after the first two hours, but it was nip and tuck at the start."

SMITH AND WADE, downcast on their return, cheered up after food and sleep and were ready to go again. On August 3, the barometer rose and they took off, circled the *Richmond* and flew out over the western side of the Orkneys. Everything went well until Wade, flying astern to the right, suddenly disappeared. Looking down, Arnold saw him make a perfect landing on top of a swell in a very rough sea. His sure touch with a plane impressed everyone at that moment. The sea was rolling with huge swells and he brought the plane down into the wind and at exactly the right time kicked it around and let it settle on the crest of a swell, and it settled beautifully. From that moment on, their biggest job was to keep the *Boston* from capsizing.

The *Chicago* followed in a diving turn, saw the oil streaking on the *Boston* and the dead propeller and circled. If they had any thoughts about landing, Wade and Ogden waved them away. Wade signaled with hand gestures that the oil pump was the trouble and to advise the patrol. The oil pressure had fallen to zero and the engine showed signs of lack of oil to the bearings. Realizing that the engine would soon freeze, he quickly landed. There were no doubts about the perilous situation. Twenty-six days of continuous fog were possible in this area and they could easily be lost forever. The sea was rising and running in cross direction from the wind. Tossing about, they were afraid to eat their lunch not knowing how long it would be before help arrived.

Smith pulled up, banked steeply, moved the throttle forward and rushed for help. He prepared notes giving the location of the *Boston*, the wind direction, probable drift and warned that the sea was increasing and the men were in danger. He dropped the first note addressed to the *Richmond* at a telegraph station on Sydero Island in the Faeroes. Arnold dropped the second toward the *Billingsley*, which was underway, and missed. He tied another note to his one and only life preserver and tossed again only to miss the deck once more. But this time a sailor dived into the cold water and retrieved the message. The *Chicago* circled the ship until it received a signal that the message was understood, and then continued to Hornafjord through rain and despite poor visibility. The destroyer *Reid*, assigned to a position halfway between the Faeroes and Iceland, was never seen. Later it was discovered that the ship was 32 miles south of its position because they had not been able to make solar observations for several days.

Wade had landed on the ocean at 10:56 A.M. Three hours later, the two men saw a merchant vessel and jumped up on the top wing and signaled with their jackets and Very pistol but did not attract attention. They waited more long hours and there was plenty of time to wonder about the outcome of their predicament. At 2:45 P.M., the British trawler, *Rugby-Ramsey*, noticed them only after Wade signaled with a pistol and rifle. This was no time for half measures. He aimed for the steel hull hoping that it would make a resounding noise. Apparently it did. As the ship came closer a voice called out, "Do you want any help?" The answer, Wade thought, was obvious.

By 3:30 P.M., the trawler had them in tow for the Faeroe Islands. The sea and wind caused continual jerking as swells alternately hit the trawler and plane. An hour and twenty minutes later the *Billingsley* came alongside and the trawler somewhat reluctantly transferred the towline. Perhaps they had a reward in mind or thought the treasure was theirs following the rules of the sea. Whatever they thought, Wade and Ogden were greatly indebted to them for their help. It may even have been a mistake to transfer the lines because these seamen knew these waters so well. Later, the State Department would forward official thanks for their aid through the British Admiralty.

Soon the cruiser *Richmond* appeared and the towline was transferred again to the larger ship. The wind had increased to 30 miles an hour in a rough sea when the destroyer and cruiser met. The men emptied the gasoline tanks on the *Boston*, took moveable equipment off to lighten the load and went aboard the ship.

With the sea and wind rapidly increasing in intensity, the hoisting of the *Boston* onto the *Richmond* began at once. It would be safer to secure the plane and start making necessary repairs. When the plane was about three feet in the air a sudden roll of the ship carried away the tackle and dropped the boom on the plane. In one destructive instant, Wade and Ogden saw their hopes slipping away after 19,000 miles. Still, they did not give up. Wade sent a radiogram to Smith from the *Richmond*:

EVERYTHING LOOSENED AND BADLY STRAINED STOP ALL WINGS DAMAGED STOP PROPELLER BROKEN STOP NEW PONTOONS NECESSARY STOP CENTER SECTION SLIGHTLY DAMAGED COMMA REPAIRS POSSIBLE STOP NEW ENGINE NECESSARY STOP UPON ARRIVAL FAEROES THIS MORNING WILL MAKE FURTHER REPORTS STOP THANKS FOR EARLY MESSAGE.

The *Boston* had taken a beating. One good thing, however, was that all supplies to repair the plane were accessible and everyone believed, or at least hoped, that it could rejoin the flight.

Fighting every inch of the way to survive, Wade and Ogden tried to disassemble the plane and take it aboard by pieces. They were two determined men, but the heavy seas finally defeated them. It seemed best to sink the plane. The aviators were understandably overwrought by such an idea and, in a last desperate attempt, Captain Cotton ordered the ship to tow the plane at four knots toward Sydero Island. It was a long shot and the towing had already strained the structure of the plane. Through the night the aircraft, like a gallant, wounded gull, rode through the rough sea. About 2:30 A.M., the captain called Wade to his cabin. He told Wade that the sea was getting rougher and that the *Boston* was slowly ripping apart. Their charts for the Faeroes were not very accurate along the rocky shores and the fog was always a hindrance. The captain said he would go in if Wade wanted to, but it would have to be his decision. Wade knew the answer. He could not risk the crew or the cruiser. He ordered the *Boston* cut loose and it was like a stab in the heart. For months the two men had lived with the *Boston* and petted and pampered her. It was a living thing, not an inanimate object. At 5:30 A.M., the waterlogged craft capsized and sank. Their deep love for the plane was real. Years later it would still surprise Wade how profoundly he felt about this lifeless object.

Wade sent another, sadder message to Smith:

PLANE THREE TOTAL LOSS RICHMOND SAILING REYKJAVIK TO ARRIVE EARLY AFTERNOON TUESDAY. WADE.

If salvage had been possible, a complete rebuilding job would have been necessary. Wade and Ogden, despite their crushing disappointment, knew that the delay would have jeopardized the success of the flight. They had simply hoped against hope. A few days later, Wade unselfishly advised Patrick not to send the reserve plane. That, too, would cause delay. His message said:

CAN ASSIST OTHERS TO COMPLETE FLIGHT.

Wade's troubles had been relatively few during the flight and now it was all over through no fault of his own. "It was a tough break after five months," he said, "but it's all in the game. We did our best." Still, it hurt. Wade went over the incident a thousand times in his mind. He could have probably made Iceland the first day. But that was no answer. The trouble was probably a sheared-off pump driveshaft that was undetectable and would certainly have broken on the way to Greenland. That would have been worse. The oil pump was the weakest link in the engine because there was no emergency pump as there was with the fuel pump. When Wade reached Iceland there were no words to convey his feelings. All he could do was put his arms around Smith. And the others shared his heartbreak.

ON AUGUST 2, MacLaren crashed in deep fog off the Komandorski Islands. No lives were lost, but the British were out of the race. No one could sympathize with MacLaren more than his American rivals, and no one could understand better than they what he had faced.

The disaster occurred near Bering Island, where the fog had dropped to the surface of the sea and the British plane, traveling at 100 miles an hour, 100 feet above a rough sea, with 100 yards visibility, missed Sealion Rock by two feet. The calculated distance and time for reaching Bering Island were running out and MacLaren knew that there was danger of dashing against another cliff. Flying Officer Plenderleith's desperation landing, along a swell in a confused sea, shattered both wing tips. They were close to land and tried taxiing to the island. As they did, each end of the lower wing alternately dipped into the sea. For two hours, MacLaren and Broome, who had been taken on when they dropped their 250 pound undercarriage, ran up and down the wing trying to balance the seesawing. It was hopeless. The plane threatened to capsize and everyone jumped into the cold surf and waded ashore. MacLaren sat down on the beach and wept. They had crashed within 20 miles of the spot where Vitus Bering, the discoverer of the sea, had been shipwrecked.

Looking back on the flight, MacLaren decided that his greatest mistake was in overloading the plane. The month's delay at Akyab had also destroyed their plans and after that everything was a battle against improvised schedules. He realized too that the lack of dual controls was a serious mistake. They would have allowed him to relieve the exhausted Plenderleith in piloting. MacLaren had followed an old British naval custom that the leader did the navigating. The Americans, of course, had the advantage of dual controls. Arnold was an experienced pilot and the other mechanics were able to relieve the pilots from time to time.

THE PROBLEMS HAD grown more complex for Smith and Nelson in Iceland. They had flown to Reykjavik where they made their headquarters in a hotel near the beach. Conflicting weather reports confused the situation. Delay was dangerous since the advancing season would become impossible for flying. Equally important for them was finding a suitable landing place in Greenland. This was still an unanswered question because of the weather. The *Gertrude Rask*, a Danish wooden ice breaker chartered by the Americans to carry fuel and other supplies, had not yet arrived at Angmagsalik on the east coast of Greenland. The ice conditions were unusual this year. The idea was to fly to Angmagsalik and then down the east coast to Cape Farewell. A flight directly across Greenland would have saved 150 miles but it was impossible. A mountain range rose to a height of 10,000 feet on the gigantic ice mass. They could not possibly fly over it with their pontoons attached.

Because the cruiser *Raleigh*'s search for an alternate base was unsuccessful and since refueling in open sea was not safe, newspapers reported that some advisers thought that it would be best to give up the flight. The changes, and possible changes, in plans told on everyone's nerves. Publicly the fliers said that this was a mere game compared with flying conditions in the Aleutians, but privately tensions grew as their destination remained undetermined.

On August 10, the *Raleigh* relayed a message from the *Gertrude Rask* that ice conditions were bad. They had been caught in the ice eight days. They would now try to get through north of Angmagsalik again but they needed coal. There was not much to do except wait and consider alternate plans. Crumrine, the advance officer, was with the two flight crews and together they studied maps, charts and weather reports. Every hour, 24 hours a day, they received radio reports with the temperature, barometric reading, wind velocity and direction, and condition of the sea. Smith, Nelson and Crumrine recorded this information on charts and traced the course of every storm.

Although the weather was moderate in Iceland, it was still a forbidding place. The volcanic island sits on a split in the earth's crust where the Eastern and Western Hemispheres broke apart and began their drift. In the 11th century, pagan Norwegians settled on this island of barren mountains, lava fields and hot springs. Reykjavik, a modern city of about 20,000 people, was the center for Iceland's fishing boats. Nelson, a native Scandinavian, found some interest in Iceland, now a separate state nominally under the Danish King. Harding said that he would have preferred a delay in Paris.

The European edition of the *New York Herald* had recently reported the proposal of a Monsieur Defrasse, a French architect, for the construction of floating islands in the Atlantic at an estimated cost of 12.5 million dollars to serve as anchorages and supply stations for planes in a projected air service between Brest and New York. The plan made sense at the time and the world flight certainly thought that one or two of those man-made islands would have come in handy.

In Washington, General Patrick became grouchier as his anxiety increased. He heard the rumors about abandoning the flight and radioed

Smith for information. Smith replied that the rumors were absolutely false, that they were in high spirits and only regretted the unavoidable delay. It may have been stretching things a bit to refer to their high spirits, but they were a long way from giving up.

Smith said that with the help of God and the *Gertrude Rask* they would leave for Angmagsalik soon. For 20 years the date that little port became ice free was about August 15. This year was different. By August 12, the old ice breaker reached its destination only to find that the landing area in the harbor was not as good as expected. The *Raleigh* sent one of their planes to Angmagsalik with Wade on board to confer with Schulze, the alternate pilot, who was now helping in the thankless job of additional advance officer. The ship had found a safe anchorage in a protected cove and the crew had attached steel cables from the bow to abutments on shore. As the plane made an approach across the ship's bow to a spot of clear water, Wade suddenly saw the cables. He shouted to Leighton, the Navy pilot, and pounded on the fuselage with one hand and pointed with the other. Leighton gunned the engine and missed the cable by inches. When the officers on board the *Rask* talked over the possible landing areas it was generally agreed that Angmagsalik was unsuitable for a base.

Schulze found a better area 15 miles away but it meant moving supplies by rowboats because the *Rask* could not break through. The flight was postponed to allow Schulze to establish the new base but weather interfered with the new plan. On August 16, the *Raleigh* reported winds blowing at 46 miles an hour with the barometer falling. The next day was worse. Schulze could not reach the proposed base with the wind, ice and ocean currents. By now, dangerous or not, Smith gave serious thought to refueling at sea.

Time moved slowly and the strain increased. Occasionally, an Icelander working at the hotel would bring one of the fliers a red rose as a silent gesture of friendship and support. In the evening the Americans would usually gather around a table in a cafe, with Navy men and correspondents kidding each other. One night the quiet Crumrine appeared for dinner in a bright red shirt that became the major topic of conversation. There was really little else to talk about. Almost nothing was said about the flight, mainly because there was little that could be said. In the absence of solid news, imaginative stories that had little relation to the facts would appear in newspapers.

Meanwhile, Bissell, the veteran of the Aleutians, had explored the west coast of Greenland with his usual care. He was now ready with a base at Fredericksdal and Smith decided to fly all the way there. It would be the longest attempted non-stop hop of the journey—825 miles, an estimated 12 hours in the air. At least, to the relief of everyone, the destination was settled.

Lieutenant Antonio Locatelli and three companions arrived in a handsome, all metal Dornier Wal flying boat and called on Smith as he waited at Reykjavik. The Italians had made no advance arrangements and hoped to take advantage of the American supplies along the route. Patrick had authorized Smith to allow Locatelli to accompany them if he believed it would not endanger success. The Americans immediately found lots to talk about with the friendly foreign visitors and enjoyed their company.

Locatelli, a member of the Italian Parliament, was an outgoing fellow who brightened up the group. Not long before he had flown across the Andes Mountains. His plane on the present flight, which appeared more modern than the World Cruisers, had been constructed for a transpolar flight proposed by Roald Amundsen which had failed for lack of funds. A new understanding emerged, with the Italian Government financing the polar plan the next summer. Locatelli was now on a preliminary flight in anticipation of the forthcoming expedition. The Wal was a central hull flying boat with two engines in tandem over the center of the wing. When Dornier, a German company, was forbidden by the peace treaty to build aircraft of that class, a company was formed in Marina di Pisa, Italy, to manufacture them. Locatelli had piloted the plane from Pisa via Lausanne, Rotterdam, London, the Orkneys and the Faeroes.

On the 18th, the American fliers were ready at 1:00 A.M. for their long flight. Loaded with fuel, the planes refused to leave the water. Tools, clothes and all other expendable items were discarded, but it was useless and in the repeated efforts Smith broke a spreader bar between the pontoons and Nelson shattered a propeller. It was almost too much. Patience strained to the limit, they now stood by for the *Richmond* to arrive with spare parts. Foreign competition was not uppermost in their minds. There was too much else to worry about. Nevertheless, on the same day, Major Zanni arrived in Hanoi and would leave the next day for Canton.

Two small holes in the left pontoon of the *Chicago* needed temporary patching with canvas and sheet aluminum. The water was ice cold and the work was miserable. The men attached a few tacks at a time and then rubbed their hands vigorously with oil to overcome the numbness. It was one more risky job that could cause permanent damage to their hands. Even their stoutest supporters were now wondering if it was really possible to fly around the world. Could it be worth it?

ON THE OTHER side of the world, Zanni had made good progress through the Middle East. By the time he reached India he passed through some heavy rain storms, broke a propeller when he sank in soggy ground at Allahabad and made a forced landing in a paddy field outside of Calcutta. Despite these relatively minor irritations, he reached Hanoi in good time. Attempting to take off on August 19 from Baehmi Airdrome for Canton, he crashed in the sodden, rain soaked field. He was unhurt, but the plane was ruined. Nevertheless, he was not giving up. Instead, he waited for his seaplane to arrive from Tokyo so that he could continue. The season was late, however, and the Argentinian Ambassador to Japan said that he would advise Zanni not to proceed beyond Tokyo. The autumn was no time to tackle the north Pacific.

TAKING OFF FOR Fredericksdal on another try, Nelson's engine cut out badly several times. He landed, opened the petcock on the front strainer and started again. Quickly he had concluded that the cut-out was caused by a slight air lock in the gasoline line. Fortunately he was right. Locatelli took off with them. The cloud base was about 100 feet above the surface and ocean swells were 25 to 30 feet. The Italians had to maintain higher speed and soon they were out of sight.

Five Navy ships patrolled the line of flight. Ninety miles from Reyk-

Major Zanni, the Argentine flyer, was another of the international
group trying to be the first around the world.

javik the planes passed the *Richmond*; 115 miles farther they saw the *Barry*, displaying a dangerous weather signal. Before long, the planes plunged into fog and 160 miles farther the visibility was so bad they could not see the *Raleigh* at all.

Running into fog and drizzle, Smith and Nelson circled lower and lower until they were just over the water. Below were broken ice and drifting icebergs. At 75 and 100 feet above the water, the icebergs were a dirty gray color in the fog. Each flier had his own thoughts about the most dangerous part of the trip. To the four men in the *Chicago* and *New Orleans*, this was the worst. They would veer one way and then another and often when they saw an iceberg ahead there was nowhere to go except up into the fog. Nelson and Harding flew alongside until Smith and Arnold turned a corner around a big mass of ice and they became separated. Finally, Smith turned to the west and found the shore of Greenland. He had about 100 miles of clear weather and again ran into fog. This time he flew over the fog and kept his position by mountain peaks. When he arrived at a peak where he thought the harbor might be he went down through the fog. To their delight they saw the Danish revenue cutter *Island Falk* waiting for them in the small harbor.

The longest and most dangerous part of the flight was over for Smith and Arnold, but there was no sign of Nelson and Harding. Smith and Arnold went about their routine maintenance half-heartedly and without saying a word. There was only one thing on their minds, the whereabouts of their two friends, and they felt too badly to talk about it. No one had to tell them about the looming dangers. They knew that Nelson and Harding were in an "aviator's hell." Had they come this far only to end in disaster? Almost an hour had passed when the unmistakable noise of a Liberty engine broke the silence. It was eleven hours and seventeen minutes after takeoff from Reykjavik. The latecomers had circled dangerously low over and around icebergs looking for a clue to a safe landing place. Nelson later said, "We just flew in every possible direction until God gave us the right one." The relief was overwhelming and, according to Arnold, they celebrated with the best party in the history of Greenland. Still, they would have felt better if they had heard from their new friend Locatelli.

When Patrick heard of the flight's safe arrival in Greenland, staff officers noticed that his disposition immediately improved. He had suffered almost as much as the fliers.

On August 24, Smith and Nelson flew the short distance to Ivigtut, a small port in southwest Greenland with the world's largest cryolite mine, where the planes underwent another change of engines before the 500 mile flight to Labrador. They were met by the USS *Milwaukee*, with Bissell aboard. During the overhaul of the planes, Nelson decided to part company with the Cincinnati battery in the *New Orleans* that had served him so well. He marveled that it had been installed in the factory and had stood up in all kinds of climatic extremes. His only reason for replacing it was that it did not come up to full charge. The generators were not always so trouble free. Sometimes they would go dead for no apparent reason.

Two days passed with no word from Locatelli. Eskimo parties searched the coastline without success and fog hampered Admiral Thomas Magruder's extensive search order. Magruder must have wished more than once that he could have escaped this mission to shepherd airmen, but the hunt continued. The *Richmond* had a belt of water 15 miles wide and 100 miles long that remained to be searched. While proceeding to take station for this purpose on the night of the 24th, a young signalman on the bridge, Seaman First Class Willis T. Pinkston, reported sighting a flare at 11:24 P.M. To his great credit, he insisted that he knew the difference between a falling star and a shot from a Very pistol. Searchlights scanned the dark sea and shortly several other signals were seen. At 12:00 A.M., the searchlights picked up the Italian plane. It was 12 miles from where Pinkston had sighted the first flare. Taken on board were Locatelli, Lieutenant Tullio Crosio of the Royal Italian Air Service and two mechanics, Bruno Fulcinelli and Givoni Braccine. The eight ton monoplane, too heavy to hoist aboard, was destroyed by fire to prevent its becoming a menace to navigation.

Seasick and exhausted, Locatelli and his crew were otherwise in good condition and glad to be alive. Forced down in the fog, they had hit the water hard, buckled the struts and damaged the ailerons so that they could not take off again. Their drifting seemed endless and the black water and eerie silence awed the stricken fliers. Each night, Locatelli had sent up green flares with a prayer. Within a few days, the Secretary of the Navy would receive through the State Department a message of thanks from Premier Mussolini for "rendering such splendid assistance." Magruder had reason to be proud of the rescue and made sure that Pinkston was mentioned in his report.

Patience, a difficult virtue, again tormented the Americans. It would have been so much easier to cast cautions aside and take a chance. But patience paid off, as it usually does. The weather cleared at Ivigtut on August 31 and the flight took off for Labrador. At last they were returning to North America. After taking off in a soupy fog, the day improved and it was an easy flight until the *Chicago* ran into trouble. The two mechanical fuel systems failed. There were three fuel systems on each plane. Only the hand pump in the rear cockpit remained and they had a long way to go. There was only one thing to do. Arnold started pumping fuel by hand from the lower tanks and transferring it to the upper tanks for gravity feed. For four hours he pumped about two strokes a minute. After the first hour his arm and shoulder became so numb that he made a makeshift sling with his belt, placed a handkerchief around his neck and pulled it with his other hand. It was tiresome, but as he said, "It beat the hell out of swimming." Later they found the mechanical gears stuck against the aluminum housing and the drive shaft twisted off.

After six hours and 55 minutes, they crossed the 560 miles of Davis Strait and arrived in North America at Ice Tickle, Labrador, where the *Richmond* and *Lawrence* plus a few fishermen and traders greeted them. The steep cliffs rising out of the ocean and the rocky, barren shore with its series of bays and inlets looked good to the fliers. Since Kirkwall they had lived with unrelenting suspense. Now the Atlantic had been crossed. After weeks of suppressed anxiety, Smith said, "Thank God we are back on North American soil."

It was another record. They were the first men to cross the ocean from east to west by airplane and this feat is often overlooked as one of the great trans-Atlantic flights. They were also the only men to have flown across both the Atlantic and the Pacific.

The four fliers waded ashore after securing their planes. Arnold was in the lead joking with the others, but he was sore from pumping fuel and couldn't lift his right arm. When they reached the *Richmond* the entire crew had assembled on deck and Admiral Magruder read a message of greeting to them from the President of the United States and the Secretary of War. General Patrick joined the welcome by broadcasting his congratulations on radio station WEAF. In the evening the aviators ate a special dinner at five, dined at six in the wardroom, and received an unexpected call to the Admiral's quarters for dinner at seven. They ate all three dinners and enjoyed each one. The ship's doctor gave Arnold a massage and a shot of whiskey for his lame arm, which was as good as new in a couple of days.

HAWKES BAY, NEWFOUNDLAND, was the next stop and from there, Pictou, Nova Scotia. At Pictou they were reunited with Wade and Ogden, who had gone ahead to prepare the *Boston II*. The plane had been flown from Langley Field by Lieutenants George McDonald and Victor Bertrandias. Despite Wade's message, Patrick had ordered the reserve plane to join the flight. The two men had accomplished too much to be left out now.

The irrepressible Wade and Ogden had already made friends with the townspeople, who had taken them to their heart. Now the townspeople looked forward to making friends with the rest of the team. There was a hearty welcome. Church bells rang, whistles blew, the Mayor and members of the town council turned out in frock coats and silk hats, the local militia wore their scarlet uniforms and the Pictou Highlanders, clad in kilts, played the pipes. There was an extra sense of joy because the fliers were late and the crowd had feared a mishap.

Sailors from the *Lawrence* riveted a plaque to a rock at Pictou, inscribed, "American aviators complete world flight." It was a thoughtful gesture, but there was still a long way to go. Ahead was the flight down the east coast and then across the continent.

On September 5, the fliers started for Boston. The dense fog forced them down and Maine, instead of Massachusetts, had the honor of welcoming them back to the United States. They landed in a well-protected harbor close to a summer colony at Mere Point. The astonished cottagers served the airmen a shore dinner of fried clams and lobsters while the grand reception with the Secretary of War, General Patrick, the Governor and Mayor waited in Boston.

September 6 was a big day for Boston and the world flight. The planes landed in Boston harbor to a chorus of guns, whistles and sirens. It was the greatest welcome since the return of the Yankee Division from France five years before. The crowd had waited a long time. Now they waited another half hour while the men attended to the aircraft. When they were ready, a gig brought the six to shore. Smith was the first out of the boat and Patrick, in his glory, rushed down the gangway to grasp his hand while the band struck up *The Star Spangled Banner*. Few could watch the scene without feeling a thrill run up and down their spine. Patrick, one of the best public speakers in the military service, enjoyed himself fully. He deserved it. His responsibility for the flight was a heavy one and all he had been able to do for the past five months was hope for the best.

A radio announcer, one of a new breed, thrust a "broadcasting instrument" in front of Smith. A radio age had begun as well as air age. In a low voice, Smith simply said, "Hello Folks—Mother I am glad to be home."

Moving through the crowd, a tall, tanned man in a straw hat and brown suit broke in on Smith, "I'm MacLaren. Thanks. Well done." It was the first time the two men met and it was only for an instant as the crowd pushed Smith forward.

With hands still dirty from work, the aviators proceeded to the State House on Beacon Street for a formal welcome by Governor Channing Cox. He saluted them as "envoys of friendship and good will to the world." Each received a sabre, silver wings and a silver bowl. From there, escorted by the 110th Calvary and the United States Marines from the USS *Cleveland*, Mayor James Curley greeted them on the Boston Common where they received more gifts, including a silk American flag. Nelson kissed the flag. He was glad to be home in his adopted land.

Early the next morning, the fliers were at the airport changing from pontoons to wheels. The elegant receptions were over and they were back to work. Lunch was eaten on a plain wooden table but there was no complaint about the menu of turkey and giblet gravy, roast beef and ice cream. By afternoon, thousands gathered to watch them do their job. The men could hardly believe that their flight had created so much interest here at home.

On the way to Mitchel Field on Long Island, the planes passed over Manhattan and had a good view of Fifth Avenue. Again a warm reception awaited them and the Prince of Wales, who was attending the international polo matches nearby, was in the grandstand. The horse loving prince, a guest at an estate in Syosset, had come to watch the British face one of the best polo teams ever put together by the United States. Under captain Devereux Milburn, were J. Watson

Webb, Tommy Hitchcock and Malcom Stevenson. But the Prince put horses aside for the moment. Besides, he was ready to collect on his bets made earlier in London.

In this well-dressed, fashionable crowd, Smith wore a brown sweater stained with grease, and the balding Nelson, "prematurely gray, wore a sweater prematurely old." It was an emotional scene and one correspondent thought that somehow the disheveled fliers made the smart-looking prince look unimportant.

In the evening there was a different kind of treat. They saw Pathe newsreel pictures of themselves, after eating dinner at the officers club.

LOCATELLI RECEIVED A wild reception in New York too, but of a slightly different sort. He took a train from Boston to New York and upon his arrival at Grand Central Station a crowd of about 5000 Italians greeted him. They were divided between Fascist and Anti-Fascist sympathizers who shouted, "Hurrah, Locatelli" or "Down with Locatelli and the Fascisti." Newspapers claimed that police reserves had to be called out to prevent a riot.

A few days later, Locatelli attended a performance of *Tosca* given in his honor. Leaving the opera house, he received a chorus of jeers as others threw tomatoes. One man, later identified as a member of the International Workers of the World, leaped onto the running board of his car with the apparent intention of assassinating him. Instead, he grappled with a detective and stabbed him slightly in the neck. Locatelli must have been perplexed by the mixed reception and glad to board the ocean liner, *Giulia Cesare*, for the trip home.

THE NEXT STOP for the American world flight was the nation's capital. Twenty miles past Baltimore, Nelson was forced down due to stripped timing gears. He made a smooth landing at Halethorpe, Maryland, quickly transferred to an escort plane and went to Washington for the ceremony. Harding was left behind to make repairs.

On the ground at Bolling Field, the President, First Lady and an

Success! Back in the States, the crew poses with the brass. From left to right, Hap Arnold, Lt. Smith, President Coolidge, Secretary of War Weeks, Wade, Nelson and Ogden.

impressive array of Cabinet members that included Secretary of State Charles Evans Hughes, Secretary of War Weeks, Secretary of Commerce Herbert Hoover and Attorney General Harlan Stone patiently waited. Billy Mitchell was there too with his spurs, riding cane and personally designed uniform. During the long wait, Secretary of State Hughes allegedly asked to be excused to attend to diplomatic appointments and Coolidge replied, "The appointments can wait." Apocryphal or not, it indicated Coolidge's attitude. He was ready to wait all day if he had to. And Hughes did not appear to be disappointed. When the planes came into view the dignified statesman looked upward with boyish interest and an enthusiastic smile. This was certainly much more fun than meeting ambassadors.

The *Chicago* and *Boston II* taxied to within 20 feet of the President. Less rushed than the last time they met, Coolidge carefully inspected the planes before everyone had a delayed lunch at the Officers Club. The patient, courteous President must have thought about the 16-year-old son he had lost that summer and how much he would have enjoyed meeting the fliers that day.

The following day the pilots paid a visit to the White House in full dress uniform. In hurriedly transferring planes, Nelson had left his hat in the *New Orleans*. He borrowed one that was too big for him and he said to General Patrick, "Chief, it won't fit me; my head is still too small."

Defense Day was September 12 and Patrick decided to keep the flight in Washington for the parade. With a day to spare, General Pershing received the fliers in the morning and in the afternoon they visited injured flying officers and men of the Air Service at Walter Reed Hospital. In the evening they had dinner with Billy Mitchell. Mitchell was a different man with the young fliers. They shared the same views about air power and the junior officers respected his position. There was no competition among them and Mitchell enjoyed the reflected excitement of the world flight. At dinner he was not playing for headlines. The arrogance and self-righteousness vanished in this company and the young men saw a down to earth, friendly, regular fellow.

On Defense Day, the three planes flew over the parade on Pennsylvania Avenue and then dropped flowers on the grave of the Unknown Soldier. President Coolidge proudly declared that day that the American defense establishment was "now, in proportion to our national power and interests, one of the smallest in the world." It was a happy, civilized boast and he pledged himself to "the purpose of keeping down to its lowest possible point the professional militia organization of the United States." In 1924 it was still possible to believe that World War I had been the war to end all wars.

At the end of the ceremonies, the world fliers climbed into overalls and went to work again. It was the same old story. A writer for *Outlook* magazine thought it should be recorded that the most notable thing about the world fliers was that "famous and yet calm, they stayed on the job." They stayed on the job because they had a tough transcontinental trip ahead of them. Almost everyone else acted as though their mission had ended. Since flights across the United States were rare occurrences, this was surprising.

After leaving Washington the weather through the Alleghenies was so bad that five escort planes turned back as the better part of valor. The mountains had been a deathtrap for more than one early flier. Yet the World Cruisers found their way through all the hazards.

A BRIGHT YOUNG journalist who had made a name for himself writing and lecturing about Lawrence of Arabia accompanied the flight across the country in an escort plane. There was plenty of competition to write about the flight but, with the help of Billy Mitchell, Lowell Thomas won the assignment. He had forced landings and more than his share of thrills, but he put together a film and narrative of the world flight and later went on a speaking tour with Harding. In Pittsburgh, as Thomas has written, there was a pioneer radio station, KDKA, and they asked him to talk about the world flight. The date was March 21, 1925, and it was the first time he ever stepped up to a radio microphone.

At McCook Field in Dayton, Ohio, the logistics center for the flight, they found many friends waiting to greet them. Dayton, the "birthplace of the airplane," took special pride in the world fliers. Besides, at one time or another, Wade, Nelson and Harding had been on duty there. Martin and Harvey were in the crowd to congratulate them on their great triumph. It must have wounded them deeply to have missed out on the mission, but they were stoics and kept smiling.

At the air base, the world fliers submitted to a physical examination on the condition that the results would not prevent any of them from completing the flight. It was a wise but unnecessary proviso. All were found to be in first rate shape.

The route across the United States was changed to avoid the high elevation of the Rockies. Their route took them to Chicago, Omaha, St. Joseph, Dallas, Sweetwater, El Paso, Tucson, San Diego and up the Pacific coast to Seattle. At each step along the way they received a rousing welcome. The crowds, receptions, banquets and publicity added so much extra work that First Lieutenant Burdette S. Wright was appointed an advance officer and he had to add three assistants—First Lieutenants R. C. Moffat and George W. Goddard and Second Lieutenant John Brockhurst. The assistants helped speed things along. At St. Joseph, Missouri, the flight landed, attended a luncheon, refueled and departed in 55 minutes.

While the flight crossed the country, *The New York Times* reported that the world flight impressed President Coolidge so much he doubted the need for future heavy expenditures for battleships. If sincere, the remark would fill the hearts of men like Billy Mitchell with joy, but even he must have suspected that this was just another way to cut military budgets.

The world fliers were glad to be home, but they could hardly wait to reach the finish line. So many things could go wrong before the end of the mission. On September 23, they arrived at Clover Field where a crowd estimated at 200,000 came out to meet them. The people around Los Angeles felt strongly that this was the real point of origin for the flight and they intended to show their special pride. The fliers probably thought this was where it all started too. An extra touch of greeting was the thousands of freshly cut roses that covered an acre of the field. To Smith it was the "greatest reception in the world." And as Nelson climbed out of his plane, he asked, "Where's Donald Douglas? He sure has built some planes." In a minute or two he found Douglas on the field.

On the flight north from Santa Monica, Wade had generator trouble and landed at a fairground just south of San Francisco. A young man driving an oil truck walked over to see if he could help. Wade told him his problem and they discovered that the truck battery could be used in the plane. The driver insisted that they change batteries and would not accept any payment. Wade appreciated the assistance and invited the young man to their hotel. That evening Wade asked him if there was anything he could do for him. His answer was, "Well, I would like to learn to fly." Wade, with the help of a public relations officer, told him to go to Riverside where there would be a letter approving an introductory flight to determine his potential. "If it works maybe we can do something for you. I'll need your name for a letter." His name was Paul Mantz. He would become one of the best known pilots of the 1930s.

The fliers reached Sand Point Field, Seattle, on September 28. Smith, Wade and Nelson landed in that order. A huge sign welcomed them. Two minutes after stepping out of the plane, Smith received a telegram from President Coolidge expressing the thanks of the country. Other messages followed from all over the world. One was from King George V of Great Britain.

Each flier received a large bouquet of dahlias and a lunch was held on a nearby yacht. It was all over. In 175 days they had flown more than 26,000 miles in about 363 hours. The average speed was about 77 miles per hour. It was a lesson in determination and courage. The *London Times* wrote, "It can hardly be supposed that there will not be fresh attempts, but the glory of being first will remain with the Americans. Nor should their achievement be judged too narrowly by utilitarian standards. The challenge thrown down by the sphericity of the earth was bound to be answered by airmen as it was generations ago by seamen. As a provocation it is like that of the North Pole or of Everest. It is a world to conquer."

IX

THE CONSEQUENCES

THE WORLD had been conquered. Was it only a stunt to grab headlines and build bigger military budgets? One cynical newspaper scornfully asked, "What did the trip prove anyway?" The *New York Bulletin* wrote, "If an around-the-world trip can be accomplished only after long and wearying delays, is the glory worth the cost?" Perhaps it was a fair question, but someone could have asked, and probably did, if Magellan's trip was worthwhile. Why did Magellan chance death in the Philippines? Or why did Drake take so long, 1046 days, to sail around the world?

In Paris, Henri de Kerillis, an aviation expert, gave the impression in the *Echo de Paris* that France had been cheated. The prize, he wrote, had been taken away after France outstripped all other nations in the conquest of the air for the previous 16 years. He did not believe that the flight had improved any techniques in the aircraft, engine or navigation. Begrudgingly he went on, "They only succeeded in reaching their end by dint of killing the motors under them and of surmounting terrible difficulties. They have shown tremendous courage and have spent an enormous amount of money . . . They have been methodical and they have had good luck, but they added nothing to the study of the great airways of the world." His criticism sounded more like a compliment.

Still, the question must be asked: Did the world flight produce any worthwhile consequences for the progress of aviation? Certainly it accomplished what it started out to do. The specific objectives of the flight announced by General Patrick at the end of 1923 had all been met. There was no argument that experience in long distance flying had been gained. It was the longest sustained flight over the greatest number of miles up to that time.

Each of the world fliers agreed that the work of the committee members and the advance officers made the difference between success and failure. At almost 80 stops along the route, the advance officers, in keeping with the original plans set in Washington, had carefully arranged landing areas, fuel, oil, spare parts and a variety of other de-

Lt. Smith landing in Bangkok.

tails to pave the way. They did their work well and it paid off. The relatively unprepared British, Portuguese, Argentinian and Italian flights all ended in failure.

The American flight was a realization as well as a demonstration that long distance flying was much more than time in the air. Nothing could take the place of painstaking planning. Some people complained about the large amount of money spent for motors and spare parts. Critics thought airplanes were too dependent upon repair and supply. And this was proven true. Complete ground organization, often overlooked in the past, was now recognized as a fundamental of flight organization, and both commercial and military aviation would require greater expenditures for that support.

Nevertheless, the ground support that the world fliers received was only the barest minimum. The pilots and mechanics did almost all of the work themselves and worked to exhaustion in the process. Flying with a mechanic in each plane had been thought sufficient to maintain the planes for the duration of the flight. It was a naive thought and far from sufficient. The system had worked only because the men were unusual. Apparently it had not occurred to the planners to station qualified ground crews along the route to relieve the fliers once the planes landed. Flight crews of the future could not operate efficiently both in the air and on the ground.

The engine, fuel system and water were the crux of most of the problems and there was no reason why they could not be corrected. The installation of pipe lines, carburetors and ignition systems were all mechanical. Nelson wrote in his engineering report that it was the small things that counted.

The Army would remain faithful to water-cooled engines for a long time to come, but their extensive plumbing was a serious disadvantage that created an overwhelming amount of work. Simply assembling the engines with more care at the plant would have saved the plane crews unnecessarily long hours for maintenance. Factory procedures for assembling and inspection required more stringent methods.

The world fliers knew how the Liberty engine had been developed. Wade, for one, said that it was a good engine considering the circumstances of its birth. All of them had a certain affection for the engine. It had given them worry and near fatal malfunctions, but it had also taken them over perilous waters, threatening jungles and dangerous deserts. The Liberty engine needed to be replaced with a more modern

Nelson and Harding loading fuel while in Bangkok harbor.

design. Still, it had served them well when a more advanced engine of that period might not have been as sturdy.

The Douglas aircraft had proven itself as the epitome of simplicity and ruggedness. It was well balanced and the pilots found it easy to handle. Everyone was amazed that the wings and fuselage had stood up so well. The materials had survived a severe test of the extremes of contraction and expansion. The steel tubing had not succumbed to metal fatigue and the varnished fabric had withstood the worst weather imaginable. The plywood pontoons, however, soaked up too much water and added too much weight at takeoff. They would have to give way to metal. In time, it was also believed that doped linen or cotton fuselages would have to yield to metal too, probably duralumin.

For now, however, it had been conclusively proven that an airplane had been built that could take the climatic extremes from Attu to Multan. Clayton Bissell, among others, thought that this was probably the most significant contribution of the world flight. They learned too that future planes operating in the tropics would have to be designed with a lesser loading per square foot to compensate for the lighter atmosphere.

Navigation had been superb on the flight, but the instincts of the pilots, especially Lowell Smith's, were probably more important than their instruments. Throughout most of the journey they kept the earth and water in sight and used the Navy and Coast Guard ships to check their course. Their earth-induction compasses seldom worked and bad weather made use of the sextant impossible when it was needed most.

Remarkably, the six fliers who completed the flight never landed to ask where they were. It must be understood that in 1924 it was not uncommon for aviators to get lost on the way from New York to Washington. The future of aviation could not always count on exceptional ability and it was obvious that improvement in navigational aids was essential.

It was unfortunate that the world flight did not use radio as originally planned. Alcock and Brown, among other air pioneers, had a radio on their transatlantic flight, but it broke down along the way. The equipment could not always be counted on, but the experience in using radio would have been invaluable. The flight clearly showed the need for an improved system of communications. No one knew better than the radio officer on the *Haida* that radio was a necessity for both routine and emergency purposes. Martin and Wade knew it too when they were forced down. In 1924, there was not a single radio station between Dutch Harbor and Japan. Now, people became aware that radio must be standard equipment on aircraft for everyday operation. Hand wig wags, thumbs up and thumbs down all had their limitations.

Radio was also needed for more scientific weather forecasting. Most of the time the fliers made their own weather briefings by checking barometers themselves, looking up at the sky and creating their own forecasts. The Navy and Coast Guard had helped, and Major Blair's analyses proved their value. Not a single day of flying was lost in Alaska through faulty forecasts. Blair gave the fliers new confidence in meteorology, but he was only one man. More weather stations and a network of professional observers who could give more frequent and accurate reports were musts. If air travel had a future it would need a weather service that consisted of more than a handful of meteorologists who worked for the Department of Agriculture. Meteorology as an aid to aviation was a scientific field ripe for exploration.

The United States had won the honor of being the first to circle the globe by air. It was a record, and records in early aviation, as now, were evidence of the ability to excel. A host of other records were accumulated along the way. It was the first flight across the Pacific, the first flight across the Yellow Sea, the fastest air time between Tokyo and Paris and the first flight to cross the Atlantic from east to west. No one could claim that they were not successful record breakers.

BUT, THE WORLD flight was much more than a record breaking event. The flight was many things. For one, it was a happy illustration of cooperation among the services. The Navy may have been envious, but their assistance was magnificent. As Lowell Smith said, "The Navy was wonderful." And his high praise was heard for the Coast Guard and Bureau of Fisheries. Also, at each step along the way the State Department was ready to give their full support.

The foreign air services, especially the RAF in the Middle East, showed a fine camaraderie for fellow pilots that transcended narrow nationalistic sentiments. Their help was freely offered and gave hope that foreign nations could cooperate in facing the problems of international flight.

The airmen aboard the fighter *Meefoo*, in Laichikok Bay.

Some observers thought that the flight showed the potential of the Army Air Service and presented a strong case for strengthening the air arm. Although Mitchell and others still looked forward to an independent air force, there seems to have been little said about the subject immediately after the flight had been completed.

Others said that the flight proved the urgency of commercial aviation. Most military aviators, both Army and Navy, believed that businessmen were waiting on the sidelines for a breakthrough that would build public confidence in aviation. In their opinion there would be no way to design and build planes or develop airlines profitably without that confidence. The world flight awakened those interests.

Donald Douglas received recognition for his part in building the World Cruisers and he realized that he had taken a big step forward in his career. His skill and imagination were alert to all kinds of commercial possibilities. He was quick to use the slogan, "First Around the World" for his company and the Norwegian government became one of his new customers. The Scandinavian country bought a plane similar to the World Cruisers, with manufacturing rights, and the planes were in service for the next ten years. By January 1925, Douglas had 500 people employed in his plant. He was now on his way as one of the great aircraft builders who led the industry between World Wars I and II.

Another instance of commercial interest occurred shortly after the flight when a group of businessmen met in Chicago with Wade and Arnold to ask questions about commercial opportunities. Ultimately, the group formed a company, known as National Airlines, that carried transcontinental mail.

In the most elementary sense, a world airway had been started. The possibilities, no matter how remote, had been shown. The trail had been blazed. Now there were facts to examine, not theories to expound. Facts replaced conjecture. There was a path to follow. General Patrick calculated that someday a flight around the world would be possible in 13 days. As he looked into the future, however, he did not believe that a world flight would ever go north to the Orient again because the weather was too severe. He thought that was one sure lesson. But as we know today, he was wrong.

Looking backward, there would not be a long gap in time between the first world flight and Juan Trippe's request seven years later for American aircraft builders to construct a four-engine flying boat capable of carrying mail and passengers on transoceanic flights. Twelve years later, in 1936, passengers would cross the Pacific in luxurious China Clippers.

A mere 25 years later, Captain James Gallagher and a United States Air Force crew of 13 would fly a Boeing B-50A Superfortress around the world non-stop from Ft. Worth, Texas. Returning to the same location, the flight covered 23,452 miles in 94 hours, one minute, with four aerial refuelings en route.

BUT, THE MOST important element that contributed to the success of the 1924 flight was the men. They had been severely tested and their intense will had won. Smith, thrust into the leadership, showed his strength under stress. Personally, each man showed a classic demonstration of determination and courage against discouraging odds. There were so many times when it would have been so easy to give up. General Patrick had every right to be proud of his carefully selected crews. It had not been a haphazard process. They had been screened and trained to the best extent possible for that day and age.

In the flight's 175 days, a genuine step forward in aeronautical science was taken. Aviation was born at Kitty Hawk in 1903. Twenty-one years later, the flying machine came of age with the first world flight. For this achievement the world fliers were often honored by airmen in the years to come and always respected. But they were largely forgotten by the general public. None of them ever became an idealized hero. Why?

One reason may be that the public had trouble remembering *one* hero very long, much less six or eight, and to make matters worse the leader's name was Smith. Still, there was a deeper public relations reason for the neglect. Within a few months after the flight, the Army Air Service would become embroiled in the court martial of Billy Mitchell. When the Navy dirigible *Shenandoah* went down in a storm in September 1925, his overzealousness led to charges that the military high command was guilty of "incompetency, criminal negligence and almost treasonable administration of national defense." It was too much to overlook and he received the court martial he had been asking for.

Whether Mitchell was right or wrong, a martyr or a troublemaker,

the trial was an unpleasant episode filled with accusations and recrimi-
nations. The Army and Navy brass were pictured as stultified men out
of tune with the times and the Air Service appeared to have too many
upstarts. Again, young airmen rallied to Mitchell's side. Both Smith
and Wade testified in his behalf. But the incident was an embarrass-
ment for everyone. Forgotten were the airmen who remained within
the system and quietly did their jobs. The world fliers were pushed into
the background while bitter headlines took over. Their admirable
achievement was too closely identified with the harsh words and the
underlying case for an independent air force. It was easier to sublimate
such reminders. Three years later, of course, Charles Lindbergh would
capture the public's romantic imagination. The world fliers, the jour-
nalists' "Magellans of the Air," deserved better.

SMITH JUMPED A thousand files ahead in the promotion list and
Wade and Nelson, 500 files. Before long, however, Wade, Nelson,
Arnold, Ogden and Harding would leave the Air Service. Promotions
were too far off. Smith, Martin and Harvey remained in the service.
In or out of the Air Service, none of them left the field of aviation.
It was a part of them.

Martin, an able officer, retired with the rank of Major General, but
bad luck plagued him. On December 7, 1941, he was the Commander
of the Hawaiian Air Force at Hickam Field on Oahu. The attack on
Pearl Harbor ruined his career. Amidst the clamor for the court
martial of Admiral Husband Kimmel and Major General W. C. Short,
Martin shared the blame. No one was interested in the fact that he
and Rear Admiral "Pat" Bellinger, commander of the Naval Arm in
Hawaii, had issued a joint report on March 31, 1941, which stated
that "the most likely and dangerous form of attack on Oahu would
be an air attack launched from carriers," and that if launched at dawn
there was a high probability of its being delivered as a complete surprise.
On August 20, Martin advised General Short that the most probable
approach of a Japanese carrier force would be from the northwest. It
made no difference. He was relieved of command 11 days after Pearl
Harbor and placed in charge of the Second Air Force at Spokane,
Washington, in defense of the northwest sector of the United States.

Sergeant Harvey had a happier career. Not long after the crash in Alaska, he applied for a commission in the Air Service. Martin, always unselfish in his praise of Harvey, wrote a marvelous letter of reference. By World War II, the sturdy, young Sergeant was a Colonel commanding a wing of the 20th Bomber Command operating against the Japanese from China.

During the '30s, Smith worked out the procedure for massed airborne landings with George C. Kenney and piloted the first plane to participate in mass parachuting. During World War II he trained heavy bombardment crews at Davis-Monthan Field in Tucson, Arizona, which he commanded. In 1945, shortly after the war, he died in a fall from a horse at the age of 53. His rank was Colonel. If he had lived, he would have probably made General. And yet, he saw himself passed over during the war as younger officers took over higher commands. It must have hurt, but he was never a man to admit it. His reserve could never be broken. When his wife brought up the delicate subject, he simply said, "Oh, I would rather be an old Colonel." But nothing could take away his courageous leadership of the first world flight.

Arnold resigned from the Army Air Corps in 1928 and joined the Maddux interests that first became TAT and then TWA. In 1940, he became Vice President of Eastern Airlines, but took a leave of absence during World War II to serve with the Eighth Air Force in England. He retired as a Major General.

Wade sold aeronautical products in South America after leaving the Air Service and made a number of pioneer flights in light aircraft, including one over the Andes Mountains. During one of his flights in South America he met Pedro Zanni and they had a good time talking over old times and comparing notes. In 1927, he briefly entertained the idea of piloting Charles Levine across the Atlantic in the *Columbia*. He bowed out after a difference of opinion with Levine; Clarence Chamberlin took his place. Wade also returned to active duty during World War II and served in Cuba. After the war he was Air Attaché in Greece and Brazil and air member of the United States Military Commission to Brazil. He retired from the Air Force as a Major General.

Ogden resigned from the Air Service in 1926 and worked at various aviation assignments. He also organized the construction of smelter and mining operations in Mexico. In 1938, he joined Lockheed Aircraft

Corporation and during the war managed all Lockheed activities in England. Later, he was Vice President of Lockheed Aircraft Service, Inc.

Nelson left the Air Service in 1926 and became vice president for sales for the Boeing Aircraft Company. By the 1930s he was inclined to think that aviation was too much of a business and much of the fun had vanished. During World War II he served as a Colonel and then Brigadier General in the Pacific and China theaters, assisting the B-29 program. He retired at the end of the war and for a time, as a technical adviser, helped the Scandinavian Airlines organize their polar route.

Harding went on a national lecture tour with Lowell Thomas—which must have suited his outgoing personality—but afterwards he returned to aviation too. He helped form Florida Airways and worked as an engineer with Boeing Aircraft and the Pump Engineering Company. In 1941, he founded the Harding Devices Company which designed and developed solenoid-actuated fuel valves used on B-29, B-32, P-82 and C-82 planes.

The brash young pilots who entered the Army Air Corps during World War II knew little or nothing about the adventures these veterans had experienced. They were from another era. Yet these men of the 1920s were the men of action who established the tradition of the United States Air Force. The older men, with memories of their youthful days, must have been bemused as they gazed upon the newcomers, who probably reminded them a little bit of themselves.

APPENDIX I

THE FIRST WORLD FLIGHT—1924

Date	Place	Miles	Time Hours	Minutes
April 6	Seattle to Prince Rupert, B.C.	650	8	10
10	Sitka, Alaska	282	4	26
13	Seward, Alaska	625	7	44
15	Chignik, Alaska	425	6	38
19	Dutch Harbor, Alaska	390	7	26
May 3	Nazan, Atka	365	4	19
9	Chicagof, Attu	555	7	52
15	Komandorski Islands	350	5	25
16	Day lost—180th Meridian			
17	Paramushiru, Japan	585	6	55
19	Hitokappu, Yetorofu, Japan	595	7	20
22	Minato, Japan	485	5	5
	Kasumigaura, Japan	350	4	55
June 1	Kushimoto, Japan	305	4	35
2	Kagoshima, Japan	360	6	11
4	Shanghai, China	550	9	10
7	Tchinkoen Bay, China	350	4	30
	Amoy, China	250	2	47
8	Hong Kong	310	3	24
10	Haiphong, French Indo-China	495	7	26
11	Tourane, French Indo-China	410	6	5
16	Saigon, French Indo-China	540	7	58

Date	Place			
18	Kampongsong Bay, French Indo-China	295	4	28
	Bangkok, Siam	290	4	2
20	Tavoy, Burma	200	3	55
	Rangoon, Burma	295	3	8
	Akyab, Burma	480	5	38
25	Chittagong, Burma	180	2	10
26	Calcutta, India	265	3	17
July 1	Allahabad, India	450	6	30
2	Ambala, India	480	6	25
3	Multan, India	360	5	45
4	Karachi, India	455	7	8
7	Chahbar, Persia	410	4	50
	Bandar Abbas, Persia	365	4	5
8	Bushire, Persia	390	4	5
	Baghdad, Mesopotamia	530	6	30
9	Aleppo, Syria	450	6	10
10	Constantinople, Turkey	560	7	38
12	Bucharest, Rumania	350	4	40
13	Budapest, Hungary	465	6	50
	Vienna, Austria	113	2	0
14	Strasbourg, France	500	6	30
	Paris, France	250	3	55

Date	Place			
16	London, England	215	3	7
17	Brough, England	165	1	55
30	Kirkwall, Orkney Islands	450	5	30
Aug. 2	Hornafjord, Iceland	555		
	New Orleans		9	3
	Chicago		6	13
5	Reykjavik, Iceland	290	5	3
21	Fredericksdal, Greenland	830		
	Chicago		10	40
	New Orleans		11	17
24	Ivigtut, Greenland	165	2	12
31	Icy Tickle, Labrador	560	6	55
Sept. 2	Hawkes Bay, Newfoundland	315	4	56
3	Pictou Harbor, Nova Scotia	430	6	34
5	Mere Point, Maine	450	6	5
6	Boston, Massachusetts	100	2	8
8	New York, N.Y.	220	3	40
9	Aberdeen, Maryland	160	3	38
	Washington, D.C.	70	1	5
13	Dayton, Ohio	400	6	43
15	Chicago, Ill.	245	2	58
16	Omaha, Nebraska	430	4	48
18	St. Joseph, Missouri	110	1	48
	Muskogee, Oklahoma	270	3	53
19	Dallas, Texas	245	3	45

20	Sweetwater, Texas	210	3	6
	El Paso, Texas	390	6	18
21	Tucson, Arizona	280	3	23
22	San Diego, California	390	4	3
23	Los Angeles, California	115	1	25
25	San Francisco, California	365	5	5
27	Eugene, Oregon	420	5	20
28	Vancouver Barracks, Wash.	90	1	8
	Seattle, Wash.	150	1	43

Total Mileage—26,445
Flying Time—*Chicago*—363 hours 7 minutes
     New Orleans—366 hours 34 minutes

Chicago is on exhibit at the National Air and Space Museum, Washington, D.C.
New Orleans is on exhibit at The Air Force Museum, Dayton, Ohio.

BIBLIOGRAPHY

Manuscript and Archival Materials

Library of Congress
  William Mitchell Papers

National Air and Space Museum
  Leslie Arnold Diary
  World Flight File

National Archives
  Army Air Service Correspondence, Reports, Maps and Other
    Records
  Coast Guard Correspondence and Log Books
  Navy Department Records and Operation Reports
  State Department Diplomatic File

Oral History Research Office, Columbia University
  "The Reminiscences of Leslie P. Arnold," 1960

Public Record Office, Kew, Richmond, Surrey, England
  Air Ministry: Air Historical Branch Records

The Air Force Museum, Dayton, Ohio
  Engineering Report, 1924 World Flight
  Frederick Martin Typescripts of Reminiscences
  John Harding Diary
  Misc. World Flight Records

The Albert F. Simpson Historical Research Center, USAF, Max-
    well AFB
  World Flight Records

Interviews

Major General Howard C. Davidson, USAF-Ret., Washington, D.C.
Lieut. General Ira C. Eaker, USAF-Ret., Washington, D.C.
Mrs. Lowell Smith, Tucson, Arizona
Major General Leigh Wade, USAF-Ret., Washington, D.C.

Correspondence

Mrs. Leslie Arnold, Leonia, N.J.
Mrs. Samuel Eaton, Ojai, California
Mrs. Marion W. Zierold, Wayzata, Minnesota

Address

Eaker, Lieut. General Ira C., "Memories of Six Air Chiefs," Squadron Officer School, Air University, June 5, 1972

Newspapers

Boston Globe
London Times
New York Herald Tribune
New York Herald Tribune—European Edition
New York Times

Aviation and News Magazines

Aero Digest

Air Force

Air Service News Letter

Aviation

Current Opinion

Illustrated London News

Literary Digest

Outlook

The Aeroplane

Articles

Baker, Ensign Lee H., as told to Admiral F. C. Billard, "The Radio Story of the World Flight," *The Wireless Age*, October 1924

Brown, Lt. Robert J., Jr., "American Airmen First to Cross the Pacific," *Current History*, July 1924

——————————————, "America Circles the Globe in the Air," *Current History*, November 1924

Christy, Joe, "That First Round-the-World Flight," *Air Force*, March 1974

Henningfield, J. R., ed., "First Around the World," based on taped interviews with Leigh Wade and Henry Ogden, *DC Flight Approach*, April 1974

Klemin, Alexander, "With the Men Who Fly," *Scientific American*, October 1923

McDarment, Lt. Corley P., "Around the World by Air," *Scientific American*, October 1924

McKay, Ernest A., "They Conquered the World," *Aviation Quarterly*, Second Quarter 1979

Wade, Leigh, "The World Flight: An All-American Venture," *Air Force*, March 1974

Warner, Edward P., "The United States Air Policy," *Current History*, November 1924

Wells, Linton and Edward B. Smith, "Weary Watchers in the Frozen North," *The Living Age*, June 28, 1924

Books

Bissell, Clayton, *Brief History of the Air Corps and Its Late Development*, Air Corps Tactical School, Langley Field, Va., 1927

Carter, Paul A., *Another Part of the Twenties*, New York, 1977

Cunningham, Frank, *Skymaster, The Story of Donald Douglas*, Philadelphia, 1943

Dickey, Philip S., *The Liberty Engine 1918–1942*, Washington, D.C., 1968

Dickman, Ernest W., *This Aviation Business*, New York, 1929

Foulois, Maj. Gen. Benjamin D., with Col. C. V. Clines, USAF, *From the Wright Brothers to the Astronauts*, New York, 1968

Graves, Robert and Alan Hodge, *The Long Week-End*, New York, 1963

Levine, Isaac Don, *Mitchell, Pioneer of Air Power*, New York, 1943

Mollison, J. A., ed., *The Book of Famous Flyers*, London, 1934

Patrick, Mason, *The U.S. in the Air*, New York, 1928

Shamburger, Page and Joe Christy, *Command the Horizon*, New York, 1968

Thomas, Lowell—As Related by Lieutenants Smith, Nelson, Wade, Arnold, Harding and Ogden, *The First World Flight*, Boston, 1925

Thomson, David, *England in the Twentieth Century*, Suffolk, England. 1965

Turnbull, Archibald D., and Clifford L. Lord, *History of United States Naval Aviation*, New Haven, 1949

Pictorial Sources

Mobil Oil Corporation, New York, N.Y.
National Archives, Washington, D.C.
National Air and Space Museum, Washington, D.C.

INDEX

3

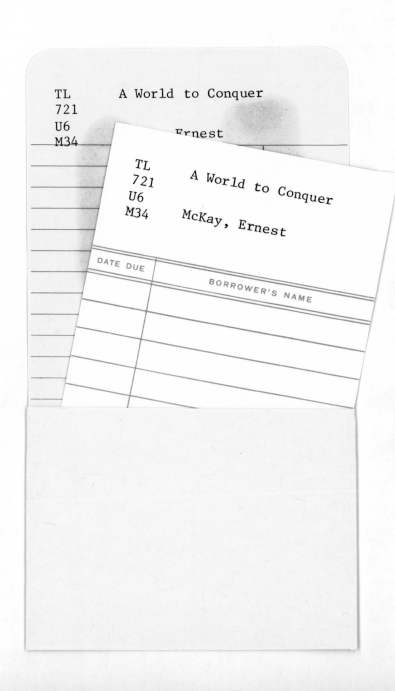

TL
721
U6
M34   Ernest

TL
721   A World to Conquer
U6
M34   McKay, Ernest

DATE DUE	BORROWER'S NAME